Betty Watk

Demetrice

Jauntia Owens

Glenda Hall

Rose Stovall

Thanks, Pastor Jeffery for your
support! Deborah Brown ...

MaryAnn Wofford — Be Blessed!

Lawaronge Davis

Lillie Jeffery

MW01488557

Ten Sisters

(Dew-Baby's)

Dew

authorHOUSE®

AuthorHouse™
1663 Liberty Drive
Bloomington, IN 47403
www.authorhouse.com
Phone: 1-800-839-8640

First published by AuthorHouse 8/27/2009

ISBN: 978-1-4490-1933-4 (e)
ISBN: 978-1-4490-1932-7 (sc)

Library of Congress Control Number: 2009908884

Printed in the United States of America
Bloomington, Indiana

This book is printed on acid-free paper.

Dedication

We dedicate this book to our exceptional and luxuriant mother, Mrs. Girstine Jeffery, who did not live to witness the completion of this book. The ten of us girls started writing it a year before her death. This is an example of time not waiting for anyone.

We also would like to dedicate this book to the outstanding legacy of ministry she leaves behind. She believed in being productive. She lived for a cause bigger than herself and used all of the gifts and talents God instilled in her to advance the kingdom of God, to help build strong functional families, and to make Disciples of Christ. She did this by precept and example. She impacted the lives of so many people, and imparted love and values to the next generation. She was the mother of twenty-two children, the church mother, and the community mother; she also extended herself to all who needed her help, directions, corrections, comfort, encouragement, and love.

To Barbara Holt Holloway, who introduced her to the world in her book, "From Cottonfields to Mission Fields". Thank you for continuing in the faith that has been demonstrated to you.

Acknowledgments

To my heavenly Father, Jesus Christ my Lord and Savior, and soon coming King, and to the Holy Spirit, my guide. "For in Him we live and move and have our being; as even some of your (own) poets have said, for we are also His offspring." (Acts 17:28, AMP)

I am grateful to my sisters who participated in writing this book by so graciously shared their stories; Jewell Wofford, Juanita Owens, Demetrice Guydon, Mary Ann Wofford, Betty Watkins, Lavarange Davis, Lillie Arnold, Deborah Brown, and Glenda Hall. Our prayer is others will be inspired and empowered from our accounts of God's faithfulness.

I wish to express my deep gratitude to my beloved husband, Elliott, for his continued love and support; and his encouragement to share this information. To our children, Derrick, Melanee, Taylor, and London; and god children, Latais Jeffery and Teresa Lee, you have expanded my capacity to give. To our eight grandchildren, who are being shaped and trained to be vessels of honor to continue this ministry of love.

I also greatly appreciate the inspiration of the committed pastors and mentors that God has ordained for my spiritual progress, the late Elder Clarence Guydon, the late Superintendent Edward Calloway, Pastor

Jewel Withers Jr., Pastor J.T. Taylor, Bishop Jerry Potts, Bishop T. D. Jakes, Betty Watkins, Pastor Fredrick Jeffery, Dr. Jim Pettit, and my current Pastors, Dr. Gene and Sue Lingerfelt. "For God is not unrighteous to forget your work and labor of love, which you have showed toward His name, in that you have ministered to the saints, and do minister" (Hebrews 6:10). And my prayer for you is that the Lord God of your fathers increase you a thousand times more, and bless you, as He hath promised you, according to Deuteronomy 1:11.

And finally, to my God given family, the Jeffery's, the Holt's, and the Toney's; and to my wonderful friends in the ministry: Ophelia Fullbright, Augusta Stout, Ruby Mays, Darian McGee, Eric Snowdon, and Lester McGraw. I pray that you continue to lift up the standard of holiness.

Preface

No matter how poor or rich we are, whether we were born in the country or the city, we live our lives according to our convictions and choices. If we have a faulty belief system, we will not make healthy choices. How can faulty belief systems change? This transformation can take place by allowing the right seeds to be planted in our lives. The Word of God is the incorruptible seed that will last forever (1 Peter 1:23). The seeds planted in us during our childhood helped shape the way we live our life today. I believe that God ordained us to the location we were born, and to the family we arrived; as a school of life. We learn our life's lessons to develop our potential. We are not afforded the opportunity to select our parents, but we are given the opportunity to know our loving Heavenly Father. He will reveal our purpose and help us to fulfill it. Joseph was sold into slavery by his brothers (Genesis 37:28). Sometimes the natural family is dysfunctional. But Joseph is a demonstration of one making healthy choices and moving from the pit to the palace. There are many exceptional leaders who came from dysfunctional families. If you come from a broken home, you could be the integral one God will use to mend the brokenness. If you allow God to use your life, He will do above all your imagination. Even though our situation seems huge, it is only a small part of the big beautiful picture God has in mind for us. Our family survived insurmountable challenges. Mother was audacious in facing oppositions, because of her faith in an unfailing God. By the protective hand of God, all fourteen biological children are alive. This is an example of the faithfulness of God.

Introduction

"A good name is rather to be chosen than great riches, and loving favor rather than silver and gold." (Proverbs 22:1)

I rode down the gravel road with my sister, Mary Ann, on Memorial Day to the cemetery. I stayed in the car while she placed flowers on several graves. I noticed the double marble tombstone. The name George Jeffery on one side and Girstine Jeffery on the other side was inscribed. All twenty-two children's names were inscribed on the back of the tombstone. Many thoughts were going through my mind as I reminisced how their story ended. What did they really leave behind? How are we living out the lessons they taught? How do we develop and train the next generation? Are we able to continue this great legacy? People in the community expect us to live up to the honor of the names of our parents. The children's names inscribed were not the names Dad called us (the 14); he had a nickname for each one of us. He called Jewell "Grandma", Juanita "Teddy", Demetrice "Ceva", Mary Ann "Maud", George, Jr. "Joe", Betty "Lou Lou", Lavarange "Vern", Lillie "Fruit Cottontale", Deborah "Bora", Fredrick "Bobwire" and "Bobbie", Rose Mary "Rooster", Larry "L.J.", Glenda "Boo", and Andre' "Big Head". We all answered to both names, however; Mother

1

chose to call us by our regular names. I could still hear Mother telling me, "Never say never", "Baby, give it to God, He'll work it out", "Gal, get back in this house and put on a slip", "Remember where you came from", "Treat people the way you want to be treated", "You'll be alright", and "I won't say what my kids won't do, but I will say, I've taught them right". To think that her voice was silent, my eyes began to run water until I thought about my nine sisters and me. Every time I am around any one of my sisters I hear Mother's voice, and I surprise myself often when I speak. It is like hearing her voice through all of us. We also have the same talents and do so many things the same way Mother did. We all have an innate sense of humor. We often respond the same way to commitments; it is really impetuous. Through the years of triumphs, joys and sorrows, Dad and Mother worked untiring hours to leave a legacy for their children and future generations. They had 14 biological children, 10 girls and 4 boys; and also raised 7 other children, the Holt's. They did not make any distinctions between the two groups of children; they treated us all alike and taught us all the same work ethic. There was a lot of love in our home, as well as, integrity, sharing, fun, closeness, and hard work.

Dad spent a lot of his time training the boys to hunt, operate the farm equipment, how to farm various crops, to cut down trees and chop wood, to fish and do mechanical work. I would carpool to work with Dad to my first public job, and he was always early. He would tell me to pay my tithes, pay myself, save 10%, and give the man a full day's work. I was so accustom to working, until I gave the man the production of three people. When I resigned to attend college, my supervisor hired three people to replace me. I was only seventeen years old and fresh out of high school, I mean really fresh, like one day after graduation when I started this job. Dad taught us all to have integrity, mostly by example. I recall most of the remarks at his funeral were about his word being his bond. One man said, "If the sun is shining, and the weather man says there is no rain in the forecast, but George says it's going to rain, I would get my umbrella". I heard creditors say, they had never known a time when Dad broke his promise. A former supervisor said

Dad was an excellent worker with perfect attendance until retirement. I thought about when I rode to Little Rock in 1976 with Dad, to test drive a new car for Mother. Dad had the salesman to call the bank in Stuttgart on the financing of the car. When the salesman hung up the telephone, he said, "Wow, that was the president, and he said to give George Jeffery whatever he wants". I was a young adult, but I knew that meant Dad had integrity and a good track record. After the funeral, we went back to Mother's house; and the living room floor was covered with flowers and plants, we counted over a hundred. The librarian came by and gave us a copy of a document that is recorded at the Stuttgart Public Library, stating that George Jeffery was a man of integrity, and a book was donated in his honor. She also was carrying a plaque to the Art Center in honor of Dad. Dad also left a tangible inheritance for all of his children; he left each one a portion of land to continue where he left off.

Mother left a legacy of the ministry of sharing the Gospel, of love, and of cooking. We would always have food to eat. Mother would cook for us, for the church family, for the community, and for every preacher and his family that came our way. The food was always good, and she never got any complaints. Mother would wake us up early in the mornings while the dew was fresh on the ground, to work in the garden. No wonder, they called her "Dewbaby", because she worked in the dew with all her babies with her. Six months after Mother's death, the ten daughters opened a small restaurant in her honor. The restaurant was opened mainly for carry out meals because of the limited seating area, but people are constantly expressing need to expand. We are closed on Sundays; that is reserved for church. We are all Christians and most of us are ministers. Mother always took us to church, and taught us to live a celibate life, and neither one of us had a baby out of wedlock. I still remember her voice when I am faced with difficult situations saying, "You do what's right, and just trust God". We are carrying out the lessons. WE ARE TEN SISTERS (Dew-Babies)!

Rose Mary Jeffery Stovall

"The Person I Am"

I arrived on this earth on October 4, 1954 and was given two beautiful parents, Mr. George Jeffery and Mrs. Girstine Jeffery. My parents believed in Genesis 1:28 that said, "Be fruitful and multiply". They had fourteen children and raised seven other children. We all lived in a three-bedroom house, which was quite a miracle itself. We were blessed to have enough food and love to be shared with one another. It was noisy around the house, but I was a quiet child.

I have been faced with much opposition, but God has been faithful to deliver me. There were times in my life that I did not think I would make it to see another day, but I have seen many more days and pray I will witness the return of our Lord. I like meeting people, and I like new challenges. During my eight year tenure with American Airlines, I traveled a lot and met many different people. I try to see the good in everyone I meet. In my young adult years, I was always involved in multiple things and on the go a lot. Mom would say, "Gal, if someone says G, you say O". I did not miss much. I remember a group of us going to different church services in the same night, until the last one dismissed. I am pretty much happy with myself. However; I am disappointed about some decisions I have made. I have learned to take the bitter with the sweet, and to carefully weigh out my choices ahead of time. I love God and value the relationship I have with Him. I work very diligently at any task I am assigned. I am a very faithful and committed person, a person of integrity, highly disciplined, and intrepid. I establish long term and short term goals for my life. I do my homework before I try to reinvent the wheel. I devise a plan and then organize steps of actions to attain my desired goals. Finally, I follow through with tenacity. Some of my friends say that I will bite the bullet. I am able to function under pressure, in fact; it almost seems normal, but I like meeting deadlines. I am the director of Dew-Baby's Incorporation. We have a restaurant where we cook home style food, named after Mother's sobriquet name, "Dew-Baby". The restaurant has only been in operation about two years, owned by ten sisters (my sisters and me).

I am the eleventh child in the birth order. Dad died January 27, 1992, and Mom died May 3, 2007. My parents were married for over fifty years and had no prior marriages. Mom had no children out of wedlock. Dad had one daughter prior to marring Mom. Growing up on the farm was a very difficult environment, because we did not have all the conveniences of the city life. We did not have running water. We had to pump our water from a well, and carry it in large buckets to the house. We would build a fire outside and heat our water in large pots. We heated our food on the inside with the use of butane burners. We did not have central heating and air, and would build a fire in the wood burning heater to heat the house during winters. Dad and my brothers would go into the woods, cut down trees, and bring back the wood. We would use electric fans and cardboards for cooling in the summers. We grew most of our food and would get up early in the mornings to work the gardens. We would cultivate the ground, dig holes, plant seeds, chop the grass and weeds down, and water the seeds. We grew our fruits and vegetables. We raised pigs, chicken, etc. for meat. Our chickens laid the eggs. Dad and my brothers went hunting and fishing for meat. We farmed cotton, beans, and wheat; and worked in the fields. Dad also worked at the rice mill at night to maintain the farm during lean times and to sustain the family. I was fifteen years old when we got our first telephone. We had a party line of four families, and everyone on that line could listen in on any conversation. We did not have call waiting; we just waited on the line until the talking parties hung up to make our call. We had a rotary telephone, and no caller ID; so we answered all calls to find out who was calling. We had a black and white TV with no remote control; we had to walk to the TV and turn the knob in order to change the channel. We only could view three channels, 11, 7, and 4. We used wire pliers to turn the knob when it was broken. When it rained or the wind blew strong, we had to go outside and adjust the antenna. We did not have video games, or computers. When I bought my first car with an eight track player, this was really an updated amenity.

Dad was a phlegmatic person. When I was young I thought he was mean due to his silence. When he came home, he would sit in the chair and watch television and tell us to be quiet. Mom stayed around the house to manage the house and all of us. She made all the rules around the house. At least, it appeared that way to us. I thought she was the authority figure in the home, because when I would ask my Dad's permission to do something, he would tell me to ask Mom. I later found out that they had an agreement not to allow us to play one against the other. Mom would drive to town once a week to the supermarkets and we would rotate turns to go with her. This was an exciting time for us. We saved the dollar we earned from working in the fields to buy something special. Mom would sew and make our clothes, but the majority of mine were passed down from my older sisters. Mom would get up early every morning and prepare breakfast, and our lunch pails for school. I was embarrassed when I saw the other students eating bologna sandwiches, and I had peanut butter and biscuits.

I had a closer relationship with Mom than Dad, and was able to talk to her about most things. Mom chastised me when I did wrong, and encouraged me when I was discouraged. I respected my parents, but I knew deep down inside that there would be a better life for me later. Mom always took us to church and taught us respect for God, our elders, and authority. I thought Dad took it to the extreme by saying, "yes sir" to younger men. We were not allowed to interrupt adult conversations. As I got older I became closer to my parents. When I was in the 12th grade during semester test time, a group of us went across the street on our break to get snacks, and we were running back on the icy road when I fell down. I slid on my knees across the parking lot while my classmates laughed at me. I got up and went to the nurse's office, and she cleaned the wounds and wrapped my knees. I went back to class and continued taking my exam. My knees started aching and blood was dripping down my legs. I went back to the nurse' office and called Mom. Shortly after I hung up, Dad came in the nurse's office and assured me that I would recover just fine. Dad took me to the doctor, and then home. I did recover just fine as Dad promised.

I started my first public job at the age on seventeen. My dad and I carpooled to work everyday. I started making his coffee every morning, and we began to drink coffee together. We would talk on the way to work about being a person of integrity. I saved my money and moved out of town to attend college, and Mom encouraged me to go. She packed the things she thought I would need. Tears were running down my face as I watched Mom wave until I was out of sight. I only had enough money for the first semester, but Mom told me that God would open a door for me to continue. I had applied for financial aid, and a few weeks later the funds came in that I was expecting. God did open the door for me to continue. I went home during the summers to work, and to spend time with my parents. Mom and I would go shopping and we would talk about my friends and my life; and the nights would be the special times spent with Dad watching boxing, wrestling, and westerns. When I decided to move to Dallas, Texas some 23 years ago, Dad assured me that I would move back to Arkansas one day. I did move back to Jacksonville, Arkansas in 1999 to help take care of Mom. I noticed that things were so different without Dad around. I said to my family that Dad was right, I did move back. Before Dad died, he asked us to take care of Mom. She had started showing signs of dementia. My sisters were taking care of her, but I wanted to contribute, because she took such good care of all of us, and the grandchildren. My family met me at my house the day I moved. They helped me move everything in, and left Mom with me. She kept getting lost in the house, because it was much larger than hers. I would see her wandering through the house, and she would say, "Oh, there you are". She was always saying, "Gal, I need to go home to see about those kids". I understood that was her life, caring for all of us. She still brought so much joy, and would say the funniest things. All of my bedrooms were upstairs, and we had a time going up stairs every night. I would let Mom help me gather the clothes, put them in the shoot to the laundry room, and fold them after I washed them. She would still let you know if the food was good or not. It was so affirming to hear her say, "Girl, that's good". We would listen to good praise songs, and Mom would move her feet and rock. She loved praising God, and would smile. I also enjoyed the environment; it was a slower pace than I had been in for the last fourteen years. In this environment my thinking was more precise. I had worked three jobs for about ten years, and had just taken an early retirement from AT&T. I was in graduate school studying counseling. I previously met with an advisor at the University of Arkansas at Little Rock to transfer my credits. After I moved to Arkansas, I was unable to transfer my credits as I was promised. I then commuted to school in Texas every week for one year, in order to graduate. After graduation, I moved back to Texas. Then I visited Mom while she lived with my sisters. My sisters would always dress her up for church the way she always would dress herself; classy suits, with the jewelry, the matching hats, and natural looking make up. She was so beautiful, and always made a fashion statement. She still loved going to church. She still realized and loved her children; no disease was able to remove that bond.

Relationship with siblings

I am next to the baby girl, and I have two younger brothers. We had more people than beds, so three of us slept in the same bed. I slept at the foot of the bed because I was younger and smaller than my two sisters I shared the bed with. We all did chores around the house, and Mother made sure of that.

My sister, Betty, was a perfect model of a virtuous woman. She would read Bible stories to us. She became my mentor, and I cried when she left home. I would go with her to visit the sick, and we would pray and clean the house. We also would go and witness to the unsaved people in the community and invite them to church. She would work on projects to help the church and the pastor financially. We would hear her teach the Word of God at home and at church.

I was not very close to my sister, Deborah, when we were growing up. She was closer to my brother, Fredrick, and would engage in daring activities. She was the smart one, but I believe she attended school a little more than I. I did know that the number of days one attended school had some barring on the grade. Deborah and I are very close now and we are able to talk about anything and laugh about our childhood. I am very proud of her. She has always been focused and has worked one job since she graduated from college. That is almost 37 years. She is such a generous person, and has been a tremendous blessing to the work of God and to so many people. If I have ever seen a ministry of giving, I have seen it demonstrated through her.

My sister, Lillie, was Dad's favorite child and he had high plans for her future. She is a good worker who does not need supervision, and is quiet like my Dad. As a child, she did not like to be bothered much. We both lived in Little Rock at the same time, and we would interact and do things together. I learned that she is a lot of fun to be around and is very witty. She is a great cook. She also has worked one job for 39 years.

My sister, Lavarange, is gregarious and has a way of lifting my spirit and is often told this by many other people. She will give her last to anyone in need. She is known to be the life of the party. She goes out of her way to take care of people, and she loves making people laugh. When we were growing up, she would rap her coat around me on cold days when we walked to and from the bus stop. She would fan us with a large piece of cardboard when it was hot. She loves people and has been labeled as the caregiver. She is the one everyone in the family calls upon when they have surgery or are faced with a serious illness.

My sister, Glenda, is the baby girl, and has been the family's baby. My brothers would treat her as if she were their baby. She is a hard working young lady, but also enjoys her position in the family. She is a beautiful young lady. I remember showing my co-workers a picture she gave me along with her two daughters, and they did not know which person was the mother.

My brother, Fredrick, is a year older than I. We took some classes together in high school, and he is very smart. In Algebra he did not study and would pass the test. We shared the same book and he seldom used it. Our teacher would get frustrated with him when he would solve a problem on the black board, because he would not follow the formula but would get the correct answer. He is an outdoors person, and is very accurate in shooting a gun. Dad trained him very well. When we were young, we would throw pennies up in the air and he would shoot holes in them. Sometimes I would ride on the motorcycle with him, but it was not my cup of tea. He would always tell me to lean in the curves, but I wanted him to slow down. He is very courageous. I remember the night he got saved; he was sitting in the back of the church when my sister, Betty made the altar call. He was holding on to the pew, but God drew him down the aisle, and he fell to his knees and surrendered to God. Later he was called into the ministry. He has been driving tractors since he was five years old. Dad would start it up, and let him cultivate the fields. He also was a race car driver and built a car to his specification. After he was called into the ministry, he participated in a race that people say he won, but he did not get the prize because the flag man said he jumped the gun. Mom said that God kept him from winning because he should have been at church. That's when he decided to give up that hobby. He married my classmate and they were married for 27 years until she died. He is remarried now, and is the pastor of the church we all grew up in. He is the one carrying out the vision of the late Elder Guydon, and has already built a new sanctuary.

My brother, Larry, is two years younger than I am. We were pretty close for a while. Larry is an honest person and admits when he needs help. He would get into situations when he was growing up by not knowing how to control his temper, and was recalcitrant. I would cry when he got a whipping. I prayed for him very much. One night I went and got him, and took him to church with me, and he gave him life to the Lord. He is now a minister of the Gospel. Larry has always been super fit and strong. He would run from his house to Stuttgart, and that is about twelve miles. I wanted him to compete in the Olympic, because he is so strong. Many of his peers call him "Incredible Hulk". Two of my students told me that they ate my niece's lunch in the cotton field, ran on the bus and locked the door. When Larry found out he started rocking the bus, and they were afraid that he would over turn it. They said that they learned their lesson, and knew that my brother was a force to be reckoned with. The doctor said that Larry was born with a hole in his heart. Nevertheless, God sure did make him strong. He loves the Word of God and can quote so many Scriptures. I remember thirty-two years ago he told me that he needed my diamond ring to get married, and I gave it to him. I guess it was a good investment, because he is still married to the same person. He started his own business shortly after he got married, and still has it. He cuts and sells fire wood, he gathers and sells scrap iron, cleans up disaster sites, farm and market vegetables, and owned a pig farm. His wife, Emma, said, "If anybody can make money, Larry can". They have one son, Larry Jr., and we call him Jay. Larry was just released from ICU two days ago. The entire medical team says he is very strong. One of them asked if he was a professional boxer. He is now in rehabilitation, and the therapists are saying that he has great strength. Three weeks ago he was finishing up his day, and working in his garden when he felt nausea. He went in the house and told Emma to dial 911. The ambulance arrived and transported him to Stuttgart Hospital. They did a CAT scan and said that a blood vessel had burst in his head, and he was transferred to the University of Arkansas Medical Center, in Little Rock about an hour or so later. When he arrived in Little Rock, he was unconscious. The doctor said he was dying, and if he did not drill a hole to relieve the head pressure immediately, then he would not make it. This is another account of God's faithfulness. I drove to the hospital from Arlington, Texas. When I arrived I saw him hooked up to all those machines, not breathing on his on; I prayed, spoke in tongues, and sang praises to our God. About four hours later, Emma called and said that Larry had awakened and pulled out the breathing tube. I went back to the hospital the next day, and asked him if he heard me having church that night and he said, "Yea" and smiled. He called me by my sobriquet name, "Rooster", so I knew his memory was good. I gave Glory to God.

My brother, Andre', is the baby of the family, and he is almost like my baby. Mom was forty-six years old when she gave birth to Andre'. He was the only one born at the hospital. I spent a lot of time with him, went to many of his functions, and gave him moral support. I was the one who stayed home with him when Mom left home for business. I met with his teachers and helped him with his assignments. When he graduated from high school, he came to live with me for a year. I helped him locate employment. He would take time with my son, Derrick. He would take him to ball games, plays, parks, and the circus. Derrick tried to emulate him and he was his role model. I moved to Dallas and Andre' tried to transfer his job, but to no avail. He joined the Army, and got married. He would write me from South Korea. When he was stationed in Missouri, I went to celebrate the birth of his son with him and his wife. He brought his family to Dallas to visit me, and he helped me move several times. He has a Bachelor's degree in criminal justices, and has retired as a Master Sergeant from the Armed Forces. He has 25 years of service for UPS, and is the Mid-South District Business Manager. He has one daughter, Andrea; and one son, Andre' Jr.

My oldest sister, Jewell, was married at my first memory of her. I did not spend much time with her growing up. She is soft spoken and thoughtful. She has one son. She was in an abusive relationship for many years, until the recent death of her husband. This is a real example of when people who themselves are hurting people, hurt other people. She always smiles, and kept going. If you did not know she was enduring such abuse, you could never tell by looking at her. God has preserved her and she has a radiant appearance. Over the past few years, she spends vacations with me. She has now retired from her job of many years at the local bank.

My sister, Jaunita, was also married when I was growing up, and has since been a widow with five children for over twenty-eight years. She never remarried after her husband's death. She has always been very ebullient, and easy to communicate with. I was close to her during my adolescent years, and felt comfortable talking to her about anything. She is obstinate and once she gets something in her mind, you can not persuade her otherwise. Mother said she was the most difficult one out of the girls to get to comply with the rules.

My sister, Demetrice, was married to the pastor of our home church until he died. She has not remarried since his death. They were married for 38 years. I have always considered her as a sanguine person. They have four children, and I was the baby sitter because they traveled a lot when the children were small. When I was fifteen years old they moved to Helena, Arkansas; where my brother-in-law was the pastor of a second church. I stayed with them during the summer to help out with the children, and I developed a closer relationship with Demetrice. I found her to be a very caring and concerned person. She is now a church mother teaching the Word of God.

George Jr., is my oldest biological brother, he was mischievous as a teenager. He would always get into trouble with my parents. I like to read, and one day I was outside reading a book, and Joe was working on his car. This car was jacked up and he had removed the tires; and by the time he went under the car, it fell on him. I ran into the house yelling for Mom, and she ran out along with everyone else in the house. We all tried to lift the car off of Joe, but the bottom part was not bugling. My brother went to get the tractor to lift the car; but meanwhile, Deborah lifted the car single handed. It was not enough to get Joe out. He was saying, "Mommy, please help me", then he stopped moving. By the time they lifted the car with the tractor, he had passed out. Mom and others put him in the car, and she rushed to the hospital. Joe had broken his collar bone, several ribs, arm, and shoulder blade. It was a miracle that he survived, and we gave God the glory for taking care of him. He usually attends my special events.

My sister, Mary Ann, married when I was eight years old, and is now a widow. She was married for thirty-two years, with one son. I remember as a child that she was meticulous about the way she dressed, and she still is today. She is very flamboyant. As a child I remember her checking everything in the mirror, layer by layer. Mother said she is prissy. We became very close and we talk nearly every day. I was away in college when she went into labor with her son. I was unaware that she was in labor, but I was feeling the pain. I was up most of the night with intensive stomach cramps. When I called to tell Mother, she told me about Mary Ann and the complications she had. Then I figured it out that I was felling her pains. We spend a lot of time together during holidays, shopping, attending special events, watching movies, and traveling. I would bring friends to her house from Texas when her husband was alive, and we would eat and bring food home. She is a great cook, and can bake many cakes like mother could. She does the baking for the restaurant and gets so many compliments.

My sister, Pearl, is older than Jewell, and was born before Dad met Mom. She is a Christian and is very kind. She lived with us along with her family during their difficult time. She also is a widow after over forty years of marriage to one husband. She is close the Jewell, and keeps in contact with the family.

The seven siblings my parents raised were all grown and out of the house during my childhood, except Earnestine, "Totsie". She eventually moved out, but never married. I lived with her one summer after she had surgery. She always embraces me with a hug and a big smile. I was close to Rosie Lee, who died in 1987. She would press my hair, bake those pies, encourage me, and always had a pleasant disposition. I had to forgive her husband for what he took her through. She could sing, and when we would go to clean the houses and cook for the sick and shut-in, she would sing "We are the missionaries, doing all the good we can". Hattie moved to Detroit when I was young, and she visits occasionally. She is a sharp dresser and is soft spoken. The youngest, Leatha Mae, died in 1989. She was married with five children and spent a lot of time with her family. Arthur, the oldest, died 2008. He would always come over with his children. I am closer to his children, because of the age difference. He always encouraged me not to give up on a good marriage. Willie Lee was always to himself. Freddie is next to the youngest and is close to the family. He is a faithful deacon in the church. He is a handy man, and is a very smart worker. He normally attends my special events.

Childhood

We were expected to be mannerly, and to respect authority. We did not question or challenge the rules. We did as we were told, and our input was not accepted. If an adult saw us misbehaving, they had permission to whip us, and when they told our parents; we would get a second whipping. Mom would say, "Don't act like you don't have any home training". When I started school, the family's reputation preceded me and all of my teachers expected me to be the class model. We were expected to practice celibacy until marriage. Mom was very strict on the dating policies, and we were not allowed to date until the age of seventeen. When we went on a date, one of our older siblings would go along, and we had a 10:00 P.M. curfew. We were not taught about sex or sexual protection, just abstinence. Most of my sisters got married at the age of eighteen, and none of the girls had babies out of wedlock. The men of the family were expected to provide for their families. It was customary for everyone to attend church.

I started working in the cotton fields at the age of six, and missed a lot of school days. During my elementary years I attended Immanuel Elementary School, which was a segregated school. We only had a few antiquated books. I was not taught phonics, just whole word sounds. I made passing grades, although; I did not learn much.

I am not easily persuaded by the opinions of others, and many would call me stubborn because I do not allow others to choose for me. Even as a child, I had very strong religious convictions and did not desire to be a participant of worldly things. My friends were my cousins, Willie Holt and Evelyn Lamb. We were members of the same church.

I ran track for the school, and competed with other schools. One year I won 1ˢᵗ place on annual track day. This was a success that gave me the affirmation that I am a winner when faced with opposition. This encouraged me to try with everything within me. I was scheduled to sing my first solo on an Easter program, and I rehearsed over and over. I was very nervous the night before, and all that morning. I remember when my name was called; I went up, closed my eyes, and sang the song, "They crucified my Lord". Everyone said, I sang very well; and I was called upon from that time to sing on many different occasions. The first school play I participated in, I experienced stage fright until I saw Mom smiling in the audience, and then I gained confidence.

My failures would be in my failing to comply with the school's rules of vaccination. I was afraid of needles used to administer shots. When I was scheduled for vaccination at school, all of the students met in the gymnasium, and I convinced my cousin to hide in the bathroom with me. We stayed until the noise stopped, and then we opened the bathroom door and saw that the gym was vacant. When we tried to quietly exit the gym, the doors were locked from the outside, and we begin to scream and holler, beating on the doors until finally the janitor heard us and opened the door. For a long time after that traumatic experience, I had claustrophobia.

My sister, Betty, has always been a very influential person in my life. I value her advice because I trust her to tell me what is right. As a child, she would take time to read the Bible to me and explain what it was saying. She lived the life before us.

During my junior school years, I went to Holman Junior High School, in Stuttgart, Arkansas. This was a different environment from the rural school I previously attended, and the population was much greater than what I was accustomed to. This was also a segregated school, and I attended this school until the 10th grade.

When I reached the 10th grade, I asked Mom if I could attend the integrated school, and she permitted me. I was the only family member who made the decision to go that year. I was faced with new challenges and worked very hard to maintain decent grades.

I entered the school's writing contest on the subject, "Why I don't use drugs", I won 1st place, and my picture was in the daily newspaper. I was the vice president of the 4H Club, and I was a member of the student council. I made the honor roll in my senior year, and it was a great year with my new friends.

At fourteen years old, I was baby sitting Andre' while Mom went to town to buy groceries. I was ironing clothes as he was strolling through the house. He broke a glass in the bedroom. I yelled out to him and he did not respond; so I left the iron plugged in to check on him. The iron cord had a short in it, and the lights began to blink on and off. When I ran back in the room to unplug the iron, a fire had started. My dad was asleep in his room with the door locked, and I managed to break the hook and wake him. I got the children out of the house and ran to Arthur's house down the road. I called the grocery store to contact Mom, and I was told that she was not there. When Mom arrived, I was walking down the road, and she asked me what happened. I explained, and then she started crying. I later found out that she was told that the children got burned up. When Betty arrived, she told me not to feel bad because it was not my fault. She commended me for getting everyone out of the house, and said the material things can be replaced, but we are irreplaceable. Her statement was one of serenity, but the whole thing was like a nightmare to me. We had to separate and stay with our married siblings until my Dad found another house.

It only took Dad two weeks to get another house, but it seemed like a long two week period. We moved into Joe's old house, and he moved to Stuttgart.

A year later, I was baby sitting Andre again. He was three years old, and was on the porch while I was in the house sewing. I asked him not to leave the porch, nevertheless; he did wander off the porch. He went by the fence, which had a tractor tire rim leaning against it, and pulled on the fence. Unfortunately the rim fell on his leg and broke it in two places. I was able to lift a 200-pound rim off his leg because of the adrenaline. I picked him up and ran to my cousin's house for help. Cousin Gracie Lamb was visiting and offered to take us to the hospital. We were on our way to the hospital, and met Dad; so we stopped him, and he took us to the hospital. I was crying all the way, and Dad kept telling me that Andre' was going to be alright. After getting Andre admitted in the hospital, Dad left to go get Mom. I called Lavarange at school. A few minutes later, Lavarange and all of my siblings came to the hospital. I spent the night at the hospital with him, but I was thinking that I should retire from baby sitting. There were just too many things happening on my watch.

Betty is still a mentor. She was away in school when I was a teenager. She would come home on the weekends, and would buy me clothes. My pastor who was my brother-in-law encouraged me to believe in myself. After viewing some of my high school artwork, he encouraged me to pursue art, and he purchased my first painting kit. He later encouraged me to get my master's degree in counseling.

Adulthood

I was seventeen when I started dating. The first person I dated was a minister. We only went to church and to restaurants to eat, and he was very respectful. We ended the relationship during our first year in college. The next two years I only engaged in platonic relationships. I was twenty-five years old when I married, and I was a virgin. I have had people to ask me how I did that. I used my time doing constructive things, and avoided idleness that caused mind battles. I also was selective of the situations that I involved myself in, and the people I involved myself with. This lifestyle was not difficult for me. Nevertheless, this marriage was the biggest mistake in my life. He had a prior marriage with children and a child out of wedlock. He was a preacher, and was unfaithful in the marriage. However; I have an amazing son from the marriage. God has a way of making something beautiful out of our ashes. I am a witness that when God adds His love, grace, and mercy to a situation; it will turn out extraordinary.

I felt that I was at a disadvantage in this area. I was taught to pray and ask God for the mate He designed for me. The older women in the church told me to observe how a man would treat his mother, because that is how he would treat me. This certainly was not true in my case. I was not told about the hidden agenda, which makes this a fallacy.

Five years later I moved to Dallas, Texas, I married a second time, and it ended in a divorce due to abuse. Four years later, I started a long distance relationship. We married and he continued to live out of state, and I remained in Dallas, Texas. I learned later the difficulties in developing a healthy relationship long distance. This marriage ended after two years. I thank God for His grace and mercy. I know that God hates divorce, and I hate it also. But I thank God that He loves the divorcee. I am glad He does not throw away His children with the dirty bath water. I went back to school after realizing my personal inadequacy in choosing commitments. I would overlook guile and not examining one's actions, and needing to be more perspicacious. I would often think people were as I am, authentic. In the past I have been too trusting. This has resulted in many unhealthy relationships. I have been a work-a-holic which is also costly to relationships. I have learned to balance things to enjoy life and not experience burn out. This is because I have learned to say, "No" when I should, and not to over commit myself. I am now married to a wonderful, hard working, Godly man, and have been since 2004. I am very grateful to Dr. Gene Lingerfelt for mentoring my husband. My husband's dad died when he was very young, so he grew up without a Dad. I can not really relate to that void. But God has given us pastors to feed us with knowledge and understanding and judgment. (Jeremiah 3:15, AMP) We are both growing in our marriage and in our spiritual lives. Five years of marriage is a record for me, and I praise God for progress. My decision to enroll in graduate school was sanction by God. This is where I met my mentor, Dr. Jim Pettit. He was the instructor in my Pre Practicum class. The first day in his class, he handed out a thirteen page syllabus; and I did everything I knew to change classes, but to no avail. Now ten years later, I know this was in the plan of God. He has provided so much insight and support through my insuperable odds. He has served as my surrogate Dad. It is through his impartation and pouring into my life, which caused me to expand my horizon and to reach new goals. What I thought was going to be too difficult, ended up being invaluable. Jeremiah 29:11 says, "For I know the thoughts that I think toward you, saith the Lord, thoughts of peace, and not of evil, to give you an expected end." I understand that we can not see the end from the beginning, but God can; and we can trust Him.

Religious Experiences

I enjoyed going to church in those days. The church Mothers would be praying, singing, testifying, dancing, and praising God. Mother would strike out on one of those old church songs like, "Take the Lord along with you, everywhere you go", "In the morning, when I rise", "Pay Day is coming after while", "I'm a solider, in the army of the Lord", "It's going to rain", "Got on my traveling shoes", "My body belongs to God", "Just like fire in my bones", "God's not dead", "Come out of that corner", "Victory is mine", "Send down the rain", "He is mine", "God is a good God, yes He is", "He's sweet I know", "I know it was the Blood", "Witness for my Lord", "Out of your belly, shall flow rivers of living waters", "Real, Real, Jesus is real to me", "This little light of mine, I'm going to let it shine", "Come on, Come on, Come on now, don't you wanta go", "You got to move, you got to move", "Don't take everybody for your friend", and "Some day I shall wear a crown". When the preacher would make the altar call, Mom would tell us to go up for prayer. She said, "You can't get too much prayer", and "Prayer won't hurt nobody". Well, we are living in another generation and I am here to say, it didn't hurt me. In fact, I would not be here today without prayer. Those Mothers were lively, and would dance until the floor would move and get dusty. There was such a freedom in the atmosphere. I am sure they had problems, but you couldn't tell by looking at them. They would tell us to take our burdens to the Lord, and leave them there. That is another song they would sing, "Burdens down Lord, since I laid my burdens down". Even throughout the day, I would hear those songs ringing in my ears.

I was taught to bless the food before eating, and to pray before going to bed. My conversion happened at the age of seven and I received the Holy Spirit at the age of twelve. I was at a church meeting during the praise and worship service. I was looking for Betty, but she was not there. I wanted her to witness my experience. I was fourteen years old when I got baptized. We had no baptistery in our home church, so I was baptized in a muddy creek, but it was a wonderful experience.

I always was refreshed during the revivals I attended. I would seek God for His will to be done in my life. I went to Church with expectation, because God was performing miracles. One night a lady was raised from the dead, we saw blinded eyes come open, crippled walking, cancer and other diseases healed, a tooth filled, a bullet popped out that was inoperable, and demons cast out of people.

I have worked with the outreach ministry most of my adult life. My greatest joy is leading someone to the Lord. I have conducted revivals and witnessed the miraculous power of God. In 1998 I went on a missionary trip to Ghana, West Africa. I was privileged to minister on several occasions, and witnessed the awesome power of God. To see packed out buildings with standing room only for all night prayer meetings was something I had never seen in American.

I worked in telecommunication for fifteen years and as a customer service specialist for three years. During my tenure in telecommunication, I remained imperturbable even when customers were filled with anger and hostility. I am a former high school art teacher, and was able to explain assignments and the students carried out the assignments. My past was a rehearsal for my divine purpose of ministering the Gospel. I have traveled abroad communicating the love of God, and witnessing to the lost, and many people have given their lives to the Lord as a result. I use parables, examples, illustrations, and gestures, to effectively communicate with others. I am an active listener, and value others input. I believe God will use our past experiences to develop His purpose in our lives. Someone said that we can learn something everywhere we go, even if it is not to go back there anymore.

I think everyone's life is meaningful, and we all have something to contribute to each other. As we develop a relationship with God, we can perfect the work and become more beneficial.

How I cope with discouragement, loss, and anger

I cope with discouragement by praying and reading God's promises in His Word. I make my daily confessions. I listen to encouraging tapes and songs. I talk to my husband, family members, and close friends.

I cope with anger by voicing my anger. I wait until I can think clearly to communicate my feelings. I develop a strategy for solving the problem, and to use my anger constructively. "A Soft answer turns away wrath, but grievous words stir up anger." (Proverbs 15:1)

My greatest losses I have experienced are the deaths of my parents. Back in 1989, I would mail Dad candy or nuts every week. Mom told me that he would look forward to getting the mail and expecting mail for me, and would ask her if her name was on it. Then one night I got the call, the call I never wanted to receive; that Dad was diagnosed with prostrate cancer. I flew home when he had surgery. The doctor informed us that he was safe, and it did not spread through the lymph node. I can vividly recall that moment, where mom and all the children rejoiced and glorified God. A year later, I received another call one night from the same sister, Mary Ann; reporting that Dad went to the doctor, and was diagnosed with lung cancer and it was inoperable. I was employed by AT&T and I called my supervisor, Shirley Thompson; and I could not believe what I was saying. It did not seem real. She asked me how much time was predicted for Dad to live. Then it hit me like a ton a bricks that Dad could die, and I started crying. She tried to console me, but at that point, I just needed time with God. After I prayed, I was able to relax and fall asleep. Dad went through treatments, and was in and out of the hospital. I would take time off work to spend time with him. I remember during the holiday season I drove to Little Rock to the hospital, and picked him up to take him home. He was discharged for Christmas, and we were so happy. On the way to the house, Dad said he was so tired of going back and forth, and it seemed like he was going in the front door and out the back door. God has a way of preparing us for things. About a month later, I had a dream that Dad asked me to release him, because he was tired and ready to go home to be with the Lord. I said in the dream, "I don't know if I can do that" and he was looking at me with such weariness in his eyes; I said, "Ok", and then let out a sigh. He looked away and up with complete serenity. Two days later, I received a call at work from Betty, saying that Dad was transported to the hospital and the doctor was calling the family in. I called American Airlines where I was employed on my second job, and all of the flights were cancelled due to a storm. I drove to my apartment in Arlington, Texas about twenty-five miles from AT&T, where I was working. I walked in the apartment and called the hospital in Stuttgart, Arkansas and asked to speak to a family member. The next voice I heard was Lavarange, and she said, "Daddy is gone, and Momma keeps saying he is still breathing". I asked her to put Mom on the phone, and she did. I told her that it was ok to release him, and I would be on the next flight out. The next flight out was several hours later. God was so mindful of me that He arranged for me to sit next to a pastor on the plane, and he ministered to me during the flight. I rented a car in Little Rock, and drove to Casscoe that night; and it seemed like the longest one hour drive that I had ever driven. It was around midnight when I arrived; and Mom just embraced me and cried. I notice that we were gaining strength from each other, but this was a very difficult time for our family.

I shared with Dr. Pettit a dream that I had in 2006 about Dad riding on a white horse, and Mom got on the horse with him. Then I asked him what did this dream mean, and he said, "You know what it means". I did, but I desired a different meaning. On May 3, 2007, I was on the freeway driving to a client's house when I received a call from my god son's wife, Kaela, and she asked, "Is it true that Grandma died?" I said, "What? I am driving, let me call you back." I called Jewell, and she asked me where I was", and I said, "I was on the freeway, but Kaela has already told me, is it true?" And she said, "Yes". I then called my husband, Elliott, and a few friends trying to keep my mind together until I got home. This was like deja-vu. I had the chore of writing reports on my clients before I left town, and it was very difficult to concentrate from cogitating on my Mom. Elliott went to work the next day, and I was home alone. I did not know when I went to visit Mom on Easter Sunday that it would be the last time I would see her alive. She was a very special lady. The next Sunday was Mother's Day, and this was a tender moment; but my son, god son and his wife went to church with me and took me out for dinner. LaTais made me an amazing plaque. He read it out loud and presented it to me. Most of the surrounding customers applauded and complimented him. Mother's name was on the TV Monitors at The Potter's House. I will always remember how supportive the church was during this time of grief, and also Dr. Pettit. Later, my sisters and I opened a restaurant in honor of Mom. We named it after her nickname, "Dewbaby's". I often wonder how Mom was able to produce such volume of work alone, when it seems massive for the ten of us. She was a noble servant of God indeed, with such grace on her life. She taught us great values; to love God, trust Him, and love one another.

Jewell Wofford

George and Girstine Toney Jeffery were my parents. They were married in January, 1939. Dad was born August 29, 1919, and mother was born April 11, 1920 in Arkansas County. Their lives changed on October 14, 1939, when a little bald headed girl, Jewellene was born. I was the first of their 14 children, then Juanita, Demetrice, George Jr., Mary Ann, Betty Louise, Lavarange, Lillie Mae, Deborah, Frederick, Rose Mary, Larry, Glenda, and Andre. They also became the proud surrogate parents of 7 other children (the Holt's) Arthur, Rosie Lee, Earnestine, Hattie B., Willie Lee, Freddie Lee, and Leatha Mae. Pearl, is my Dad's daughter prior to marrying my mother, which makes her the oldest. Yes, we are one big happy family.

I was born in Casscoe, Arkansas. We were raised on a farm. We grew most of our food. We had cotton, rice, soybeans, corn, peas, peanuts, sweet potatoes, and a large garden with all kinds of vegetables. We had hogs, cows, goats, horses, chickens, turkeys, ducks, geese, and genies. We only had to go to the store for things like flour, sugar, cornmeal, salt and pepper. We all worked very hard. Dad was a great provider. He would hunt, fish, and trap for meat. He never came home without his prey. So we always had food. Mother was a great cook. She was very creative, and was able to make a meal out of nearly nothing.

We have always gotten along with each other really well. Leatha Mae was about 17 months older then I, and mother always dressed us like twins. Every time a new baby was born into the family, Dad would say, "one more won't hurt". I started walking about 9 months old, and I was so fast learning things. My Dad's mother, Grandmother Maud Lillie Jeffery, said that she wanted to live to see me at two years old, but she died before I turned two years old.

The first school I attended was Mt. Pisgah in Casscoe, Arkansas, and that site is presently a cemetery. I missed many school days because of the long walk. One day my classmates and I were shaking a limb on a tree, and it hit me and knocked me foolish. I still have a scar between my eyes from that incident. I later moved in with my Grandmother Myrtle Toney Pike, my mother's mother, and attended school in Lookout, Arkansas until I completed the 3rd grade. I then went to Immanuel High School, where I graduated.

By me being my mother's oldest biological child, I learned to cook, clean, and baby-sit as a young child. My sister Lavarange started walking at 15 months old, so I carried her around. I remember taking her and my younger siblings to doctor's appointments.

In the summer we pitched metal watches for fun, and played checkers in the winter. Dad made us a checker board on a wooden box, and we used the soda pop tops for checkers. God gave dad so much wisdom. He made us a playground, entailing a see-saw from a barrel and wide board, a swing from a rope, and a merry-go-round from an old wagon wheel. We had so much fun. Because of the size of our family, we always had enough of us to play any kind of game. We loved playing basketball and baseball. One time Dad carried all of us to the movie theater in Stuttgart to see "the globetrotters", and we were ecstatic.

In the 1940's it would snow heavily in the winter. We would make snow ice cream and it was so good. My best friend Ruthie M. Browley, witnessed to me about Jesus Christ, and received Him and was filled with the Holy Ghost. In 1953, at the age of 14, I joined Mt. Calvary COGIC where I am still a member today. Elder A.J. Pendleton was the pastor then and he lived in Palestine, Arkansas. He would ride the greyhound bus to Roe, Arkansas, about five miles from the church and walk the remaining distance. We only had one man member of the church, Brother William Wofford. So my aunt Lillie Mae Bryant, my mother's sister, would drive the pastor back to the bus stop. Mother got saved and joined the church after I did. She was a very faithful member, and became a church mother. She started preparing Sunday meals for the preachers and others, beside her large family. She was a good and faithful mother of the church until she became disabled. The church was about three miles from our house, and we would mostly walk to church and were excited about going, it was always so good. The church mothers could really sing, and we would get in a hurry when we could hear them singing and praying. The church played a tremendous role in our upbringing, and we attended on regular basis.

I remember how hard we had to work to retain the farm. We had to chop and pick the cotton. It seemed like an unending job. When we finished our crop, we had to help Grandpa Eddie Jeffery chop and pick cotton. As if that was not enough, we would go and work in the fields for the community farmers, and then we made money. My Grandpa's mother was Nancy Nobles, and his dad was James Jeffery. They married in July, 1882. Nancy was a Cherokee born in Jackson County, Alabama. She moved to Casscoe, Arkansas in 1895, along with her two sons; Ben and Eddie Jeffery. She was very nice, and would take care of me when mother had a new baby. She died on December 28, 1947 right after Christmas. My Grandpa was born in 1895 in Huntsville, Alabama. We would look forward to the times when Dad would take us to Grandpa' to watch TV before we got our own. We would love to watch Amos and Andy. Then Mother would take Grandpa to his doctor appointments and help take care of him. He died October, 1980.

We did not have central heating and air. We would gather wood to build a fire for heating purposes. In 1954, my sister Juanita and I were walking along the edge of the woods picking up brush to make a fire under the wash pot, and a rattle snake bit my leg.

I thought I had been struck by a thorn, until I looked down and saw the snake crawling away in the weeds. Juanita ran to the house and left me behind. By the time I made it to the house, mother sent my brother George Jr. on his bicycle to go find Dad because he had the truck. God really gave Mother a lot of wisdom, and she tied a cloth tightly around my leg over the bit. Dad came and off to town we went to the doctor's office. We lived about eleven miles from Stuttgart. When we arrived at the clinic, the doctor rushed and cut my leg where the bit was and put it in a pan and the blood jelled. Then the doctor said, "My that was a poisonous snake". He did not think I would live, and told Mother to bring me back if I made it through the night, but God was with me. The only thing I could think about was missing church. When we got home, Mother sat by the bed all night and prayed. The next day Mother and Uncle Buddy carried me to the doctor's office, and he said, "You are lucky, oh well, somebody's got to be lucky. I didn't think I would see you again." Of course, I knew that God had spared my life, and I thank God.

I was unable to walk for a while, so I could not attend school. But my classmates were so informative. They would send me lessons and all of them would write me, and that was nice.

I enjoyed my high school years at Immanuel High School. The classes were small, and we were like a family and related to each other very well. One of my favorite classes was Home Economics, and Mrs. A. Jones was the teacher. We would sew, cook, and learned etiquette. The girls would prepare dinner for the boys, and invite them to eat with us. The boys would take Shop classes while we were in Home Economics.

My class graduated May 22, 1959, with only 32 students. We were glad and sad, because we were all so close and we hated to go our separate ways. It was like a family breaking up. After graduation, I attended Delux Beauty College in Pine Bluff, Arkansas. Aunt Puttin sponsored my trips home, so I went home every weekend. I got a lot of practice doing hair for my family. I graduated from Delux in 1961.

I started dating Arlanders Wofford, and he was also from a large family of 9 boys and 4 girls. On November 4, 1962, Arlanders and I got married in the front yard of Uncle Buddy's and Aunt Puttin's house.

In 1963 Aunt Puttin got sick, and had kidney failure. She passed away and went home to be with the Lord. We were all very sad, but we knew that she went to a much better place; because she loved the Lord. We would prepare dinner and have family gatherings. After I got married Dad would come by and pick me up to go fishing with him. He taught me how to fish. I loved going fishing for my pass time, and sometimes I would go with my mother-in-law. Dad started calling me grandma, and many family members still call me that. We had our only child, Reginald; on December 15, 1965. I was pregnant at the age of 26; at the same time Mom was 46 years old and pregnant with her baby boy. My baby brother was born on January 27, 1966. Demetrice and Juanita were also with child, and they both delivered in July. These boys grew up like brothers. They started school at the same time, and did sit side by side, with the teacher not knowing that they were related until the end of the day. The teacher said she knew that was not going to work. I always wanted a girl; so God blessed me with two lovely grand daughters, Neaka and Rekenya. Neaka is 22 years old, and a senior in college. Rekenya is 12 years old, and in the 7th grade. My daughter-in-law, Kawanda is a lovely girl who treats me like her own mother; and she calls me Mom.

In 1996, my son Reginald and Kenneth Avery started a business together named, "Kenreg Inc." They do excavating, including backhoes, tracking, dozer dump trucks, top soil, and gravel. They also have road trucks, they started with five trucks; and they both drove trucks and managed the business. The business is very successful, making over a million dollars in 2005.

In 1974, I started working at Farmers & Merchants Bank in Stuttgart, Arkansas, where I was the first black employee. I was a vault teller, and retired in 2004, after 30 years of service.

Dad had a short battle with lung cancer, and requested that we take care of Mom because she had started having transient ischemic attacks (TIA). Dad went home to be with the Lord in 1992. And we did take care of Mom, we kept her in our homes until the last year of her life, she lived in Demetrice's home under hospice care. She went home to be with the Lord on May 3, 2007.

Arlanders owned Corner Inn and Wofford' Soul Food Restaurant. After my retirement, I did all the baking in the restaurant. He did really well, and worked hard. He had a stroke on September 20, 2007, and they had to care flight him to a hospital in Little Rock, Arkansas; where he remained until his death. He passed away on October 12, 2007. My sister, Lavarange, witnessed to him gave the invitation to be saved. He accepted Christ as his personal savior during his last two weeks stay in the hospital. I was glad of that, because the next week he was unable to talk plain. He kept muttering something, but I don't know what. God is a merciful God. I don't advise anyone to wait until they are on their death bed, because I may be too late.

Juanita Owens

I am the second child of 14 children. As a child, my Dad's day would begin around 4:00 A.M. He would trap and hunt meat, while my mother would be busy in the kitchen putting together a meal. She was a great cook! Many of her recipes were passed on to family members. She did not use measurements like many traditionally use today, instead she used vague descriptions such as "A hand full of this," "A pinch of that," and "Pour until it looks like it's enough." Mother always prepared a good meal to feed all twenty one of us and we often had food left over.

We had a variety of food in our garden; peas, beans, greens, tomatoes, okra, lettuce, onions, squash, corn, reddish, sweet potatoes, peanuts, watermelons, cantaloupes, honeydews, and other vegetables. We also had apple, peach, plum, pear, and fig trees. So there were always options to pick from when it was time to eat.

As the sole provider, my Dad was a man of few words but he was seasoned with grace, love, and he was always kind to his family. Fishing was his favorite hobby.

My Mom was full of faith in God. She allowed God to lead her on how to care for her family. She would work the gardens and canned much of the food for the winter. We would all work every day except

Sunday because mother would take all of us to church. In addition, mother was a hard worker for the church.

We were a very close family. However, because we did a lot of things together I was much closer to my sister, Demetrice, than any other family member. Mother always said, "Gal, you are so stubborn." I thought I was pretty compliant but even today some still say that I am stubborn. When I was young I was a very strong fighter. Boys or girls, it did not matter because I would fight both! Growing up, my Mother, my sisters – Jewell and Demetrice - and my pastors were my role models.

I have been a widow since 1980. My late husband, Mack Lawrence Owens, and I were married for 19 years. One night he came home and opened the refrigerator door and had a massive heart attack. He fell on the floor in the kitchen with his eyes open. I as well as all of our children was in the house. I kept calling his name but there was no answer. We lived in the country about 15 miles from the nearest town. I called 911 for an ambulance to come from Stuttgart and when the paramedics arrived, they transported him to Stuttgart Hospital where he was pronounced dead on arrival. He was only 39 years old. This was the worst day of my life. I kept thinking, "Oh Lord, what am I going to do?" Suddenly, I saw our world crumble right before my eyes. I now had to be both Mom and Dad. I did not work at the time. I was a house wife. My husband preferred for me to take care of home while he provided. Our children were teenagers when he died. Sherry was 18, Evonda was 16, Tonia was 15, Lawrence was 14, and Beatrice was 13. We were all in a state of shock. I had so many unanswered questions and so did my children. Mack was a great provider and he was a very pleasant and kind man. We had just recently returned from a vacation. He won a car and tried to convince me to purchase a new vehicle. I did not drive much during those days. Mack would always take me anywhere I wanted to go. He was very supportive in everything I did. He did not attend church but he would drive us to church service and drive back to pick us up. With five teenagers in the household, Mack's death threw my life into a tail spin. I found myself carrying the load and doing my best to fill the void. I washed the clothes, earned the money, cooked the food, did the repairs, nursed the wounds, transported children to different functions, went to the schools, wiped the tears, corrected the mistakes, and helped with homework. My days were filled with chores and many concerns. I could not have made it without the mending love of God. He helped me keep us together as a family. We were faced with overwhelming challenges. In 1968, Tonia was diagnosed with having a virus that caused her to dehydrate. She was taken to the hospital and the doctor had to put IV's in her head and body to hydrate her. She looked bad, her head was sunken in, and the doctor said that they had done all that they could do because her body was still rejecting fluids. He then shook his head and said, "I am sorry." I could not believe my daughter would die because my faith in God was strong and I knew that He was the Healer. I called out to God to touch my daughter. Suddenly, Tonia began to open her eyes, move her arms and feet, and make noises. When she was examined later, there was no brain damage and all of her vital signs were fine. The same doctor that shook his head and apologized earlier stated, "She is a lucky little girl." But I knew that she was blessed and that God healed her. There was another incident with Tonia when she was washing clothes during a thunderstorm. I remember so well that I was reading Psalms 91 in my Bible when I heard a loud clap of thunder that shook the house. There was also a bright flash of lighting. I knew that something was hit so I ran through the house checking. As I ran through the house, I found Tonia unconscious on the floor of the wash room. I picked her up and the electrical current was shooting through my body, but I could not put her down. We took her to Stuttgart Hospital where she was admitted and the doctor said that the current was still in her body. He would have to wait before giving her anything. He did not want anyone to go near her. After a few days of monitoring Tonia, the doctor said that he could not understand how she was still alive because of the large amount of current in her body. The doctor said she was blessed that the current went down her body instead of up her body. I began to thank my great God for His miraculous power. He has been so good to me and my family. Despite the trials that we went through, God was always with us. He brought us through every time.

I thank God that all of our children, Sherry Pickett Owens, Evonda Owens, Tonidaia Glover, Lawrence Edbert Owens, and Beatrice Jackson are supporting themselves now. Beatrice has a Bachelor and a Master's degree in Business Management from the University of Arkansas at Little Rock, Lawrence has a Bachelor's degree in Business Administration from Southern Arkansas University at Magnolia, Evonda has a Business Education certificate from Rice Belt Vocational Technical School in Stuttgart, Sherry has a Business certificate from Phillips Community College of the University of Arkansas, and Tonia received a Cosmetology license from Steve Earls Cosmetology School in Stuttgart as well as an Associate of Arts from Phillips Community College in Helena. They all continued their education so that they could provide for their families. Beatrice and her husband are doing so well that their house was featured on the cover of Real Living (Arkansas Home style Gardens Design) Magazine. The importance of going to school continues in my family. I have three grandchildren who are currently in college. I have never heard my children complain about going without. They made it without a Dad in their adolescent years; and as young adults, they still remember what their Dad taught them. Their Grandmother also spoke into their lives and greatly impacted each of them.

My Spirituality

I received the Lord Jesus Christ as my personal savior and was filled with the Holy Ghost at 14 years old. It was a wonderful experience and it brought a change in my life. When I was saved Elder Andrew Pendleton was the pastor of Mt. Calvary Church of God In Christ (COGIC).

He was so faithful and determined.

Pastor Clarence Guydon was the next pastor and he was a good leader. He was the pastor for 37 years when he died on January 20,

2001. He was a Bible scripture person and a prophet. I still see some of his prophecies being fulfilled today. After Pastor Guydon died, Elder Joe Davis was appointed pastor of the church. He was a loving and faithful person. He worked to fulfill the vision Pastor Guydon had on constructing a new building but he died in 2004.

After Pastor Davis died, Elder Fredrick Jeffery became the pastor of our church. Pastor Jeffery is carrying out the vision, and has finished the new church building. He reminds me of Pastor Guydon when he teaches the Word of God. He always says, "I got verse and Scripture." God has really given him wisdom, knowledge, and understanding to lead the church.

I began working in the church with my Mother, and she trained me in many things. Now I am a church mother, the distinct president of the YWCC, and a Sunday school teacher. Previously, I was crowned mother of the year. My Mother taught me to be faithful in the midst of life's trials. She always said, "Give it to God, He will work it out". This thought is always with me. I know that God sees all and knows all. I only see a small part of His plan but He sees the whole plan and works it out for me. I know that He loves me. When I think about how He has been there for me, I find peace that surpasses all understanding. So with all things, God knows best.

I like to read, fish, and attend church service. I like good inspirational books to read. I find fishing very relaxing for me, and I got good teaching from dad. In my earlier days, I went with dad a lot. I very seldom miss a church service, I am considered as part of the faithful few. I will be there when there are only two or three in attendance. I enjoy the outdoors and taking care of my plants, and I still live in the country. I also enjoy spending time with my family. I have supported my children in caring for the grandchildren when needed.

Demetrice Jeffery Guydon

I am the 3rd child, born April 7, 1943. When I was born Mother was 22 years old, and Daddy was 23 years old. Dad passed away in 1992 and Mother died in 2007. I was born and raised in the country in the deep south of Arkansas County, Arkansas. I am a mild tempered person. I don't like to fight, and the few fights I have engaged in, I saw no alternative. I always choose the way of peace and like to give people the benefit of the doubt. I have been told that I make excuses for people. Growing up I had a problem confronting issues, but now I am straight forward. My family members say if you do not want to know the truth, do not ask me. I am 5' 7" tall and after I got married, I gained a lot of weight. I have been working to lose weight, and have lost 55 pounds.

When I was about 10 years old, I went to live with Mother's sister, aunt Puttin and her husband, Uncle Buddy. They did not have any children. They were so good to me, and both of them would give me lunch money and food to take to school. I remember sharing with other students. I did not like the cats they had in the house, because they would get on my bed at night, and I would sleep with my head under the cover. Aunt Puttin would take me fishing with her, and we would walk about a mile through the woods to the lake where she would catch fish. Later that evening, we would walk back in time for her to cook for my uncle, and sometimes she would walk back to continue to fish. The first time we went fishing, my aunt did not take any thing to eat. I told her I was so hungry that my belly was flapping together, so she started bringing snacks and drinks along. She was such a good cook. She made the best homemade ice cream.

One night I left church with a group of friends who lived across from the church, after that my aunt told me not to go over there. While I was playing, I fell and cut my knee. It was sore and I bled for a long time. I still have a scar. My aunt cleaned and nursed the wound, but I learned my lesson. After a while, I started missing my siblings, especially Juanita, so I moved back home. Things were a little different at home, because I had another sibling.

My family is very friendly, we laugh a lot, and most of us are charitable. Our parents taught us to share. We had a lot of fun growing up. We would play hop scotch, horse shoes, honey-honey-bee-ball; hide & go seek, jump rope, play house (cooking mud pies), treating our dolls like real babies, we made dolls using grass for hair, and we built a big round tin play house. I was so proud of the results because we put a lot of time and care in it. We played in the yard so much until the grass did not grow. Many times mother would call us inside because we would play until it got dark, and we did not have street lights. Mother made us a yard broom, and we would sweep the yard and keep it clean. During fall seasons, one of our high lights was going to Stuttgart to see the Circus. The Circus only came to town once a year. Then years later, the Fair would come to town, with rides, games, and food. I really like the polish sausages with mustard, relish, and onion. The pink and blue cotton candy was good, and so the buttered popcorn. We would walk up and down the side walks looking for people we knew. We would stop talk or stand on the corners and eat popcorn.

Lookout

Lookout is a small little rural area with a population of less than 100 people. Almost everything is located in a curve, with two country stores and two clubs. Our great aunt, aunt Cool, lived there. She was a great cook who made some of the best food one could eat on a wood burning stove. On our visits there, we would play volley ball with the neighborhood children, and make trips to the store. Although, this is a small community, it was a popular place, until the older people died, some moved away, and the stores and clubs closed. Then it seemed like a ghost town. There we're more than 50 people left. Aunt Cool lived until she was 103 years old.

We started out with kerosene lamps, smoothing irons, and hand fans. Before we got electricity, we used card boards, hats, and whatever we had to fan with. 3 or 4 of us slept in the same bed, and it was so hot in the summers. My sister, Lavarange, was so compassionate that she would sit up in the bed and fan all of us, while she would be dripping in sweat. I remember when we first got electricity, a TV, an electric iron, and electric lights, we were so excited.

Our family celebrated Christmas, New Years, and Easter. Mom would bake enough cakes and pies to last until the New Year. We would cut our own Christmas tree. During the holiday season was the time we would spruce up the house. We would paint, buy new furniture, rugs, and do a general cleaning. We were taught about Santa Clause, until we found out differently.

We chopped and picked cotton, carried water from a barrel to wash clothes on a rub board and hung them out on a clothes line to dry. In the winter time, the clothes would freeze on the line. We had a hand pump that you had to pour water down to prime to get water. We would sometimes wander off and explore the woods. We enjoyed finding and eating the heckle nuts, muscadines, and skater bars. They were very good. I think Mom marked me by a squirrel, because I like all kinds of nuts. We would kill and roast black birds over an open fire.

Dad had a mild mannered horse named Kit, and a wild mule named King. We would rub and play with Kit, but we did not bother King. Kit was brown, and King was black. We had goats that would get on the roof of the storage house and eat the clothes off the clothes line. It seems like they would eat almost everything in sight. Beside Mom and Dad, Jewel was the only one who learned how to milk the cows. We did learn how to churn the butter from the milk. We would place the milk in jars, secure the tops, and shake until butter formed. The hardest animals we had to control were the hogs. They would break the fence or root under the fence, and get out. Dad had to round them up, and put them back in repeatedly. We had one big white one who tried to attack Dad when he tried to corral him. We were afraid of him when he was out of the pen. Dad finally had to kill him. Among the chickens we had, there was a fighting red rooster. As soon as we would go out the door of the house, he would start strutting toward us, getting prepared to jump on us to peck us. We were afraid of him, and would run. Mom had to kill him also.

Dad would also trap furs. He knew how to cure and preserve meat, and we would help. Mother was a very creative cook. She believed in keeping us clean. She said that she would carry 2 or 3 changes of clothes for me when she took me places, because I loved playing in the dirt.

I remember being fascinated by my cousin's car. I was playing with the door. Dad told me to stop, but I was disobedient, and my cousin did not see me and closed the car door on my little finger. I think it broke because it is crooked today.

Mother would leave me in charge of watching the food when she went to the field. Because of my compassion, I would feed my younger siblings part of the food if they were hungry. When Mother returned, I would get in trouble for giving them part of the dinner. I have always been a hard worker. Mother would stop me from cleaning the entire house because she wanted all of us to share in the work.

During the harvest time for the wheat and oats, we went to the fields after the wheat and oats had been cut, we gathered straw to make our own mattress to sleep on. We had to be careful how we placed it, because if we pressed against the stubble it would hurt. We were excited to sleep on the mattress right after we finished making it, because it was full and high. One day we were gathering straw; Joe sneaked up behind me and jumped on my back, knocking me down in the stubbles. I was so angry with him; I chased him but did not catch him. He ran on top of the hen house and laughed at me while I threw rocks at him.

I had a difficult time learning how to ride a bicycle. My siblings would hold me up and spontaneously push me, but I would still put my feet on the brake. Due to the fear of falling, it took me a long time to learn.

A typical day in the winter time, Dad would usually get up before us to make a fire or to rekindle it. I recall going out in the cold many times to gather up kindling wood for the fire. I also would go outside to the pump to get water for us to get ready for school and to drink. Mother would rise early to cook breakfast. She would always make homemade biscuits, syrup or rice, eggs, and home cured ham or bacon. Some of us would get up early and get dressed for school, while others would lie in bed until the last minute and be rushed to get dressed in time to catch the bus. We had to walk about a mile to catch the bus. Our bus driver, Mr. Saul, was very patient with us, and he would wait on us to arrive at the bus stop. As soon as we returned home from school, we had to change clothes, do our chores, do our homework, and then we could play outside. When Mother called us in the house supper would be ready. I can not remember eating anything that was not good. We took turns washing the dishes and cleaning the kitchen. Our bedtime was 10:00 P.M. on school nights.

Mathematics and English were my favorite subjects. My sister, Juanita, and I were always close and graduated at the same time. I graduated from Immanuel High School in 1961. I was a member of the Honor Society, and I graduated Salutatorian of my class. 30 years later I went to Phillips county college and got a Certificate in Computerized Accounting, and I graduated with a 4 point average.

My Dad was raised in a Pentecostal church, and Mother was a Baptist. I became a Christian at the age of twelve. Mother received the Holy Ghost a little before I did, and after Jewell. We would work in the fields and talk about the church services. We could hardly wait to walk three miles to the church. I really like hearing the sound of the organ music. I am intrigued about the things of God.

History

After I graduated from high school, I moved to Stuttgart and started working for Stuttgart Hospital. One night at a church meeting I met a handsome veteran, who later became my husband that next year. We moved to his home town, Clarendon, and started our family. Victor was our first child, and he died of crib death four days after his birth. This devastated me. My husband did all he could to comfort me, people prayed for me, but it took God to help me deal with the pain, and to give me the strength to go on.

My husband became a minister of the Gospel. He was very faithful to the church and to his pastor. He later was appointed pastor of Mt. Calvary Church of God in Christ, the church I grew up in. It is amazing how God had been preparing me for this. Even when I was a child, I would tell my siblings that God did not like for us to lie and act ugly and they would listen. My husband was the pastor for 38 years until he died in January 20, 2001. The church gave us anniversary services every year, and treated me like queen for a day. They would give us money, food, and gifts of appreciation. One year someone gave us a cow, a dryer, a microwave, living room furniture, just to name a few. My husband was a great Bible scholar and great teacher. He was known for exemplifying the wisdom of God. I am teaching more in our church now than I was when my husband was alive. I teach adult Sunday school, youth classes, and in the general service every first Sunday. We are living in part of my husband's dream. His dream was the new church building we now have. He also had a vision for a youth center, and a retreat center for the elderly who have dedicated their lives to serving God and others. A place where one could come, relax, and recuperate.

I learned that a house is not necessarily a home, but God needs to be the head. My husband was the priest of our home. When we were confronted with problems, he would confront them. He spoke into our lives and encouraged us to pursue our destiny. He always told us not to settle for less than the best. We would work together in our home, and when two people work together for the same purpose they can accomplish much more than an individual. When a home is out of order, you have chaos that will affect everyone involved. My husband spent many hours in prayer and studying the word of God. He spent relentless hours traveling conducting revivals throughout Arkansas, Kansas, Texas, and Milwaukee. The weather did not get too bad for him to go. He said that God told him that if he regarded the clouds, that he would not prosper. He was so faithful to his calling and many people were blessed, healed, saved, and filled with the Holy Ghost. People still tell me about the things they learned from his teachings, and how the prophecies he gave came to pass. The things he taught me enhanced my life, and increased my spiritual growth. I miss him so much. I treasure the things he imparted in my life and what we shared together. However, I know that he did not want me to grieve. We believe to depart and be with Christ is far better.

In 1966, I gave birth to our 2nd child, Veronica, and we were so excited. She was so fast and brought us a lot of joy. Then in 1968, Jonathan was born. He had such a heavy voice and would sleep a lot. In 1970 Mary Elizabeth was born, and she was a jolly baby who would laugh a lot. Then five years later our last child was born, Charles Harrison, and he got into everything he could.

Mary Elizabeth and her husband have four children. Their oldest son just graduated from high school. They have a set of triplets, two girls and one boy. I regret that my husband did not live to see the triplets, they were born in 2002, and he died January 20, 2001. They tell me that I live too far away, because they live in Lincoln, Nebraska.

Jonathan and his wife have one baby girl, and my husband did not live to see them get married, nor the baby. Presently Veronica and Charles are single with no children.

When I was pregnant with my oldest daughter, mother and two of my sisters were also pregnant at the same time. Mom was pregnant with my baby brother, which was her last child. My parents had 28 grandchildren and 58 great grandchildren.

We did not go on vacation when we were growing up. After I married we started going on vacations. We went to beautiful Hawaii for two weeks. One of the most exciting trips was to Disney World in Florida, the children had a blast. I was excited to see their faces light up when they entered Disney World and saw Mickey Mouse. My daughter and grandson from Nebraska flew in and met us there. However, my grandson had chicken pox the day of their return, and was not allowed on the plane. So they had to stay over two extra days and see the doctor before they could return to Nebraska.

My first train ride turned out to be a disaster. First of all, it was three hours late. Veronica and I were traveling to Lincoln, Nebraska, to see Mary Elizabeth deliver her triplets. Due to the initial train being late, we missed our connection at the change location. The train went to Chicago, Chicago was not in the schedule, so we had to spend the night, and catch another train the next day. Needless to say, that we missed the arrival of the triplets. I have not desired to ride a train since that time.

I worked in direct sales for Princess House for a few years, and I met a lot of people. I traveled to Louisiana, Mississippi, Chicago, New Jersey, Kansas, St. Louis, and throughout Arkansas. I won a two week vacation to Hawaii for two, me and my husband.

One thing I really regret is that I was not taught how to budget or save money, so I spent all the money I received. And if that was not bad enough, my husband was not taught either, so we made such a big mess with our finances. We were like too big adult accidents going somewhere to happen. However, I was not satisfied with our financial conditions and wanted to be more responsible. I was determined to live debt free. It took several years to accomplish and with the help of the Lord I am now debt free. I regret that my husband passed away before it happened. I am now teaching all of my children how to live debt free. I taught them to budget, save money, and pay cash for what they buy. They are amazed at how much this system is helping them become debt free. They have the extra money to pay their houses and other debts off early because this will save you a lot of interest. I have always tried to honor my appointments and show up on time. I respect the time of others.

I under went a major surgery, and had a traumatic experience. I was bleeding to death. The doctor kept giving me blood, but it was constantly passing through me. The doctors had given up on me, and put me in an empty room with no machines. When my husband was informed, he ignored the do not enter sign and walked passed the medical staff were I was and prayed for me. My husband said that I had changed colors and looked very pale. At that point, the doctor thought about 'Avatin', a drug that has only been used once, so he used it on me and it worked. That's been over 30 years ago and I am still here. Thank God for His grace, and giving the doctor the wisdom. I know God gave me my life back for a reason and I will serve Him forever. I have been in three automobile accidents as a passenger and I sustained only minor injuries.

Although I moved away from the farm Dad bought and we grew up on, I ended up moving back. I now live a few yards from where I grew up; and I love it here. Seven of the girls are still members of the same church we were brought up in.

Daddy taught me how to fish. Once I caught a 23 pound buffalo with a telescope pole with a bream hook. He gave me a fight, but with the help of my sister, Lavarange, we landed it. I enjoy fishing and it is so relaxing. I went rabbit hunting when I was about 12 years old at night with my brother, George Jr., (Joe) when he was 11 years old. I carried the light, and Joe, carried the gun. It was kind of a scary experience, but we returned home without a rabbit or anything. My Daddy also taught me to drive a standard shift truck. I thought

I had learned pretty well and offered to help Dad out, so he would let me drive my siblings to the cotton fields. I could not control the speed. When we had to cross a high bridge I would almost bounce my siblings out of the back of the truck. One of my sisters asked if she could get off before I cross the bridge and let her run and catch up after I crossed the bridge, and I did. I thought fast driving was good driving. One day my cousin let me drive his car and I drove 90 miles an hour on a dirt road, and I lost control trying to make a right turn into the yard. The door flew open and it scared me, so I begin reducing my speed; even to this day I have never received a traffic ticket.

My parents had a pretty good rule system because Dad was gone so much; working, hunting, fishing, etc. When he was home we would ask him if we could go somewhere, he would always tell us to ask Mom. We already knew Mom's answer, but we were hoping his answer would be different from Mom's. We were unable to trap him. Dad taught me to shoot a gun and we would go target shooting. I got so good that I would rarely miss a target. Dad was a very accurate shooter, so were all of my brothers very accurate. They all like to hunt. Dad would let me shoot his riffle. One day my brother, Joe, played a trick on me. He convinced me to shoot his gun, which had a kick back and it was so loud. When I looked around at Joe, he had his fingers in his ears. He was so mischievous.

I have feet and hands like my Daddy, so my hands and feet are larger than the rest of my sisters. This was good, because the rest of my siblings could interchange shoes and get hand me downs, but I did not. In my school days, I remember wearing laced up high top shoes. We were glad when they went out of style. To my amusement, they came back in style, I still have two pair. Mother would sew and make our clothes. I made most of my children's clothes, and I also made clothes for other members of the family.

In 2006, Mom was in hospice care, and moved in with me. Lavarange also moved in to help care for Mom. Mom improved tremendously for over a year. May 2, 2007 Mom passed away at my home. It was a privilege to help keep her comfortable, during her final days on this earth. She helped raise most of the grandchildren, and she never refused to keep any of them.

Mary Ann Jeffery Wofford

I was born September 19, 1945 in Almyra, Arkansas. I am the 5th child and the 4th girl born to Girstine Toney Jeffery and George Jeffery. My brother, George Jr. is eleven months and twenty-five days older than I, so we were very close growing up. He was my playmate. As a child, we played a lot outside and did almost everything together. We were just like twins. We had our own games, such as honey-honey BB ball, Hide and Seek at dusk, Ring around the Roses, London Bridges, Hop Scotch, and Jump Rope. We had pet pigs that we would take turns riding. We had so much fun. I would play with my dolls alone, using the Johnson grass for hair, combing and plaiting it. We would find mud holes and practice swimming in them.

Every time Mother went in labor, Dad left and came back with the mid-wife, Ms. Mary Jane. She was always carrying a black suitcase. I knew we would get a new baby, because we thought she had one in the suitcase, but we learned better. Jewell was like a second mom; she did a lot, and would take all of us to the doctor for our shots. Once, a patient at the doctor's office asked her if we were all her children. She was only a child herself.

When I was growing up, I remember the Holts, living with us. Earnestine never married, so she was still living in our home when I married and moved out. Rosie Lee had twins, Milton and Mildred,

47

during my childhood. My brother, Joe and I asked her to give them to us, and she agreed. Although she was not serious, we went and got paper bags to put them in. When they moved away from the house there was not a segregated school in their area, so they ended up living with us in order to attend school. This caused us to become very close, and they seemed much like siblings. I remember Freddie and Leather Mae (the youngest) living with us. Jewell is the same age as Leatha Mae. Arthur was the oldest, and was married to our step grandmother's daughter. They lived about a half mile down the road.

The Mitchell family lived about a mile from us and owned the county store. Prior to getting our own television, Mrs. Ella Mitchell would allow us to join her family and watch the Saturday morning cartoons. They had two sons, Troy and Tommy, and we would watch cartoons with them. They began to seem like family. I will always remember those special times we shared together. I started working in white people's homes as a teenager. I would ride with them to the home on the back seat, and today it is called chauffeur. When we arrived at the home, I had to use the back door except for the Mitchell's. We all entered in the same door. We did not have a telephone, but the Mitchells had one. If mother had any urgent call, Mrs. Mitchell would walk to our house to deliver the message. This speaks of her character. I had the opportunity to inform her how much I valued her kindness, and appreciated all the things they did for us. She said that she appreciated my family as well. She said that George and Dew Baby helped them by shopping at the store. She could always depend on what they said because they were loyal to their words. Mr. Lester, her husband was also kind and nice.

We did not have running water inside. We got our water from a pump outside that we had to prime and pump for water. There were times when all of our efforts failed. The pump did not produce water, so we would carry water by hand, or push it in our little red wagon from the neighbor's house, which was a mile away. We would put tubs and buckets out to catch rain water to wash, and to bath with. We bathed in a round tin tub, and then later we progressed to a long tin tub where we could actually stretch our legs out. The process was that after the first person bathe, then the next person in line would bathe using the same water. I guess the first child was the clean one.

The laundry was done outside in an iron wash pot. For the white clothes, we would boil the water and use a tin wash board to scrub them by hand. The white clothes would get so white and bright. We would hang all the clothes with clothes pins, on clothes line to dry. In the winter time, often the clothes would freeze on the line and we would take them in the house to dry them behind the wooden heater. Dad was always cutting wood with a long hand saw, and we would carry it to the house in our little red wagon. We had plenty of trees from the woods around us, but we had various uses for wood. We would heat our flat iron on the wood burning heater and press our clothes, before we got electricity. Our cooking stove was a wood burning stove. We did have oil lamps to provide light as we would read. Dad read a lot of western books back then. Reading became one of my hobbies. Although we all worked, went to school, and played outside. We all were home at night enjoying the family. We could count the stars at night in the sky and they seem to have been much brighter then, than now.

We thought we were rich when we got a lot of hand me downs. We always got new clothes during the winter months after the crops were harvested. Mother made sure we were dressed for the occasion and the seasons. We had the high top shoes, rubber boots, sweaters and caps, and the striped overalls (black and white with flat buttons in the back) the cute fashion I hated. Oh I can not forget the long johns. We went bare footed around the house during the summers. The summer times were special and we would have a huge picnic by the lake in the woods, of course, we had to catch fish, clean them, and fry them in a big pot. We had other foods like home made ice cream.

Mother required us to keep our straw and feather mattress fluffed and neat and to make up our bed daily. I remember her bed was a great example, with white ironed sheets and starched pillow cases. Although her room was off limits to us, we could see the bed when the door was opened. We had wooden floors, but not like the modern day wooden floors. Our fan was whatever we could find to use, by hand of course. We had an outdoors toilet; of course, it was a little double wide wooden house. Yes, we did have some privacy.

We had a smoke house where all of our meat was preserved and kept in a smoke meat box, with lots of salt. George Jr. and I would get in the box and eat the salt. I will never forget the time when George Jr. got his hand caught in the big trap set for unwanted animals or rats. I run in the house to get Mother to get his hand out of the trap. Thank God for His mercy, there was no broken bone. We had a hen house where the chickens would lay their eggs. They laid white eggs and brown eggs. Dad would build a straw container in the ground to keep the sweet potatoes in. We would let the peas and peanuts dry to preserve them through the winter months. We would pull the whole peanut stalks up, and then pull the peanuts off the vines after they had dried. Then we would bake or cook the peanuts with butter and salt. During the winter, this was our snack as we sat around the wood burning heater for family time.

When Dad brought our first bicycle, he told us to share and take turns. Dad instructed us not to ride anyone on the back of the bike, but Deborah was crying to ride on the back, so I let her ride with me. I just could not say no to her. Well, while she was riding, her foot got caught in the wheel and injured. Mother had to take her to the doctor, and I felt so bad. Besides, I knew Dad was going to get me. This taught me a lesson not to disobey my parents. When Dad made it home, he sent Joe and me to the cotton field to work, which was better than getting a whipping. Dad only whipped me twice in my life and I have never forgotten. Most of the time I would obey, but I took a lot of Joe's whipping. He was so spoiled being the only boy among eight girls.

Mother would feed all of the children first, and she and Dad would eat last. Every morning she would make pans and pans of biscuits, by the dozens. I really don't know how she made so much desert, cakes, fruit pies, cobblers, and jelly. We did a lot of walking and running and didn't have any weight problems. Dad grew sorghum cane. He would cut it, put it on the wagon, and carried it to the mill where sorghum molasses was made. It was very sweet and delicious. We didn't spray insecticide over our crops, so we did not worry about the chemical damages. We would just pick figs off the trees and eat them right from our back yard, and they were good.

I remember Dad hunting for deer, rabbits, squirrels, ducks, geese, and quail, in the winter times. He would do a lot of fishing in the summer. He would trap minks and coons at night to sell the furs for extra income. He would put a carbolic acid light on his cap for lighting.

I remember one day Freddie was working on his car. He put some diesel fuel in a jar and set it on the porch. Bobbie was young, and he thought it was green cool aide; so he dranks the diesel fuel. He started changing colors, and Freddie realized what happened and told Mother. Mother was speeding for sure, getting him to the doctor. God spared his life, and this was a miracle.

I was five years old when I began picking cotton with my siblings. We could pick two bales a day. We had the reputation of picking more cotton than anyone around and were called, "the cotton pickers". I eventually got up to picking 357 pounds a day. I was so proud of myself, and so was my Dad. Dad would carry the cotton to Dewitt, Arkansas, to the cotton gin where he was paid by the pound. When Dad got paid for the cotton, we would then get our allowance of $0.25. We looked forward to going shopping and only worked until noon on that Saturday. Of course we had to take turns, because we did not have a bus large enough for all of us to ride together. We did pick and sell plums, berries, figs, and muscadines. We kept all the money we made from the sale. In 1957 our cotton crop was very productive. Dad purchased a new blue and white ford. People were saying that we were rich. We just had a blessed year. Somehow God always came through for us. We were so glad to get on the back of that truck to ride to town. We had to travel a mile down the dirt road each way, and I am sure we were all dusty when we got to town. We were so glad to go to town that we didn't care about the dust. This was during the time of segregation when there were signs saying, "Whites only". We had a different water fountain to drink from and different restrooms to use. We would shop at the five cent and dime store, and the whites were waited on first. We parked at the bus station, and that was our social place. The boys would hang out there and the word was out that the country girls were coming to town. Our parents would shop down town at the grocery stores, and clothing stores on rare occasions. We all had to stay together. Even as teenagers, we were not allowed to be alone. Sometimes Dad would bring back groceries after he went to the cotton gin. These were special times, because he brought candy,   cookies, and lots of good things for children.

I went to Immanuel School in Almyra, Arkansas. I missed a lot of days of school during the harvest time, but I managed to get my lessons and make up the test. We had split sessions and summer school, to allow us to be out during harvest times. I loved school, I was an honor student, and graduated with honor. Our school was rated A, and we had wonderful teachers, who taught us about life. Math was my favorite subject and I received the best math student certificate, along with Billy Wilder, who was the valedictorian. This was quite an accomplishment for me, because I was not the smartest student in the class. I was the devotional leader in our home room class. I guess I was perceived as the most religious one. We would begin the day with prayer and songs. I learned many practical things in home economics; like house keeping, cooking, grocery shopping, planning meals, and sewing. Reading was one of my hobbies, and I think I read every book in the library. When it was time for a book report, all I had to do was decide on which book I wanted to use. This knowledge has taken me places I've never thought I would go. These lessons have played a big part of my adult life. In my early adulthood, I sewed and made all of my clothes. I made suits for my husband and son. I made many of his' and her' suits that really looked professional. I was nominated as 'best personality' for four years. I also received a scholarship, but did not think my parents could afford to pay the remaining expense, so it was not used. I was proud of my achievements, and I made my parents very proud. The students were bussed from DeWitt, Gillett, Ethel, and St. Charles. We could hardly wait to see the new students arrive. The teenage girls would check out the new boys. The milk man would bring fresh cold milk to the school for the students in the little glass bottles. We had big glass bottles of fruit drinks, and we redeemed the bottles for cash.

I didn't know but one of my grandparents, and that was my Dad's father. He had cotton fields, we always worked for free, and we never got paid. As a child, I didn't understand. My older sibling would work for community farmers for money, while George Jr. and I would pick cotton for Grandpa Ed without pay, because we were too young to go with them. George Jr. would play sick so he could go home, and I would do the same, because I was not staying out there alone. At times I did feel sick, but as soon as I got home I was totally healed. Oh well, what did he expect, we were just kids that didn't get paid any money. I did not know any of my other grandparents. They died when I was a baby or before I was born. Mother's sister, Aunt Puttin, was like the grandmother I never knew. She was so good to us. She did not have children, and wanted mother to give her at least one of us. Mother said that she would just let us spend nights with her. She would always bring us food and make us homemade ice cream. When she got sick and was in the Hospital in Little Rock, Arkansas (University Hospital) by me being the oldest girl at home, I had to go with mother and spend the night at the hospital with her. Mother was so sad and they didn't think she would make it through the night, but she did. I was praying she wouldn't die while I was there, because I was afraid. Thank God she made it through that night. Family members came over and picked us up the next day. By the time we made it to our uncle's house in Stuttgart, she had passed away. I was in the 11th grade, and this was a very sad time for me. I had never experienced anyone dying who was that close to me. It was in the winter and snow was on the ground the day of the funeral.

Christmas & Teenage Years

Christmas was a huge celebration for us. We always went into the woods; found our Christmas tree, drug it home, and decorated it together. The entire room had the aroma of cedar. Mother would start baking a few days before Christmas, and we are still keeping this tradition going. As a child, I would always get one toy and it was no surprise because it was always a doll. We all got a stocking stuffed with apples, oranges, hard candy, whole coconut, and fire crackers. When we got old enough and didn't believe in Santa Clause, we did not get any more toys, which was no fun. One Christmas I picked up a fire cracker that George Jr. lit but did not fire, and it went off in front of my eye. Mother took me to the doctor; but there was no permanent damage, so eventually I was alright. But up to this day, I don't like fire crackers.

I received Christ at an early age, and was raised in a very strict church, Mt. Calvary Church of God in Christ. My favorite services were Sunday school and Y.P.W.W. I was a Sunday school senior teacher. Joe and I often conducted the praise services by leading the congregation in songs. Zelotis and Esnolis Wofford would also lead the praise services a lot. We grew up in this church, and I am still a member today. I am the Y.P.W.W. president; I serve on the Broad of Directors, and I am the Church Missionary. The church had so many rules and regulations, we were forbidden to go to ball games, dances, and wearing pants. So I never went to a Prom or anything, and students would make fun of me, but I learned not to let it bother me. I had my own mind and took pride in standing up for what I believed in. I wanted to live for the Lord and didn't think I missed out on anything.

During my teenage years, I would work in the homes of white people cleaning and baby sitting. I made good money, and bought my own clothes. I have always taken really good care of my clothes. I wash them by hand in cold water, and hang them outside on the clothes line. I still follow the same procedure today. Mother always wanted us to look our best when we left home, and many people would say that I look like my mom. I think this is a compliment, because she was a beautiful lady, and always dressed so well. Although I do think I have ways like her, I think she was more beautiful than I. When Joe became a teenager, we stopped hanging out together. Instead, I started hanging out with Mother in the kitchen, and cooking with her until I left home.

My cousin, Tillie Lamb, became one of my best friends. She lived about a half mile from my house. We would walk to the school bus together, play together, and we attended the same church. My best friend in school was Jeweldine Warren (Hall). We remain friends today, and she is one of the nicest people I know. She is the most unselfish friend I have ever had. Whatever she had, I had it also, because she would share with me. I see her from time to time, but we do have telephone conversations; and we support each other. I love my friend, Jeweldine. I have always had close male friends, they have proven to be very trustworthy, and not sharing your secrets. I feel free to discuss anything with them. They have always respected me. I believe this has a lot to do with me being so close to my brother, while growing up. I do remember mother telling us not to take everybody for your friend.

Adult

Shortly after I graduated, I married James Vernald Wofford, after dating him for two years. He asked mother for permission, because that was the only way I was going to leave home. Mother give him permission, and then we had to get my Birth Certificate; only to find out it had Mary Ann Jeffery and I had been using Maudestine Jeffery. I was happy to comply from that point, and later my last name was Wofford. Originally I was named after my grandmother and mother. My grandmother was named Maude Lillie, and mother was named Girstine; so Maudestine was a mixture of the two names. I guess the mid-wife couldn't remember what name to record or couldn't spell it, with limited transportation and no telecommunication; my name was recorded Mary

Ann Jeffery. We did not know this until I was eighteen years old. I do know that Maude means God's Gift. After getting my name right, I started planning my wedding. This was a big event, on the front porch of our house. I was all dressed in my wedding attire, with the family's passed down wedding dress; worn by all of my older sisters. Mother made the wedding cake, and the minister, Elder Collins was also our professional photographer. I remembered being so nervous after the wedding was over, because I had to leave home. I had been so sheltered. I was use to my older sisters going along everywhere James and I went. Now I was on my own, and I didn't have a clue how that was. James had rented a small house in Stuttgart. The houses were close together, and I was not use to that at all, so I pretty much stayed in the house. The people were very friendly, and we had a store in our neighborhood. We went grocery shopping the next day, and we had $10 to spend. We bought everything we needed for the week. This was our weekly budget amount for groceries. James worked on a farm in the country, and I spent my days at home. I remember that $1.00 would buy four gallons of gas. I started riding to the country with James to work on my dad's farm. We had a car, but I didn't have my driver's license, nor could I drive well. I had to get use to the environment in town; it was noisy, and the trains were loud; waking me up every morning at 5:00AM. I was use to the rooster, but not the train. We did not have a television or a telephone. I started walking downtown to meet family members when they came to town. I started working in different homes for income. I was then recommended to be the bookkeeper for Dodson Plumbing Company, and I worked there for a year. Mr. Charles Dodson was a very good boss, but I decided that I wanted to have my husband's dinner ready for him when he got home, being the great house keeper that I am. So I went back to being a house wife. I would set the table appropriately and serve dinner out of the serving dishes; not from the stove out of the pots and pans, and I enjoyed doing this. We then moved into a larger house in the same neighborhood, and we were happy to have more space. After a year and a half, we purchased land in the country and build a house, where I live today. I was so happy because it is only a couple of blocks from the Church I am still a member of, and the houses are not close together. We were so proud to purchase our first home, and to be around people we grew up with. We both had a good relationship with our in-laws. I did some domestic work. I like this neighborhood. We would get together every Wednesday and go groceries shopping for bargains at different stores. Some stores gave redeemable green stamps. My husband was enjoying our new neighborhood. It was closer to his job, so he started coming home for lunch. I enjoyed preparing three meals a day as much as he did. He was providing for us. We had a washing machine with a ringer, and no dyer. I would hang the clothes on the clothes line. In 1969, I was shopping at Safeway Grocery Store, when the store manager offered me a job. I was so surprised, and told him that I would let him know. At this time, they were picketing a Kroger Grocery Store across the street from Safeway. When I got home, I asked James if I could work for Safeway, and he said, "No, we are doing okay". He did not want me to work outside the home, but I told him that I really wanted to give this job a try; so he finally agreed. This was during the time of the civil right movement, and I was the only black working in the store. Many whites did not want a black person to check them out at first, of course, they did not say black. I didn't feel good about this, I knew I was not working for them, I was working for Safeway. I knew that God would get me through this, and I knew I could do the job. As time progressed, most of them came around and were glad for me to check them out; in fact, some of them became good friends. This shows how God can change things, and change people. I am glad that I didn't quit, because I had excellent benefits; a union, a credit union, a retirement plan, and an excellent health care plan. I will never forget my first pay check; I could not believe the amount, because I had never made that much money before. God really blessed me with that job; I was later promoted as head of the department. Then I was offered a position as store manager in another city; I declined because James didn't want me to drive out of town, but I was honored. In 1975 my son, James Samuel Wofford, was born. This was one of the happiest times in my life. My first child ended up being my only child. I only gained seventeen pounds during my pregnancy, and everything went really well. My delivery didn't go well, the doctor had to induce labor, and I was in labor for 27 hours, then I had to have a cesarean. Mother was the one who violated the security limits at that point to tell the doctor that I could not have the baby, and please give me a cesarean. I finally had a fine little boy, but mother said I did not need any more because it was too hard for me. I guess mother knows best, because he is the only child. I returned to work after three months, and mother was my babysitter. James was very helpful in taking care of the baby; because we had been married about ten years before having a baby, everyone spoiled him. My co-workers and customers were very excited for us. Later Safeway built a new building in Stuttgart. We were advancing and making good money. I was promoted to Retail Manager, and had to attend classes in Little Rock, Arkansas. I was enjoying my position, and I also was the File Maintenance Manager. In 1986, Safeway suddenly announced their closing due to bankruptcy. This was such a shock; I had enjoyed working for Safeway for sixteen years, then I was unemployed. I drew unemployment until it was gone. Then I was job searching, and was very disappointed over the minimum wage pay offers. I had been accustomed to making a lot more money than that. This was the onset of trials; James had surgery and was not working, so we had no income, and the bills were piling up. One day Riceland Foods Incorporation called me, and offered me a part time position for minimum wage. I accepted because it was better than nothing. I started working on June 10, 1987, and that same day my father-in-law was hospitalized and died. This was a day I will not forget. Immediately after my work shift, my sister Deborah gave me the news about James's dad. When I received my first check, it looked like a one day pay check. I remember thinking; I worked all week for this. Nevertheless, I am still working for Riceland Foods Incorporation, because I am not a quitter and I believe that things will improve. I know that everything will not always go my way. After six months, I was promoted to full time after a co-worker retired. However, this was not a pay increase. I still made minimum wage for three years. After two supervisors retired or moved on, my present supervisor reviewed my file, and discovered that I was not receiving the correct pay, so my pay was corrected. I thank God for every step of improvement. That was over twenty years, and I still have the same supervisor. I have great respect for him. Meanwhile, Samuel was growing up, and he loved school and was very active. He was an honor student, played basket ball and played foot ball, sang in the chorus, ran track, and was a boy scout. He received the Eagle Scout Award along with other recognitions. I was proud of his accomplishments. James started working for Rice land foods in 1981, and he really did like his job as a Fumigator, until he injured his back. After he had three back surgeries, he was disabled. He was closing a box car door on a train, and the door jammed causing injury to his back. This happened July 5, 1989, and he had his first back surgery September 14, 1989. The second surgery was on September 13, 1993, the last one was February 11, 1997. He kept working until 1997. He was never the same after that, and he missed his job so much. Then he had other health problems; difficulty breathing, sleep disorder, emphysema. He was using an oxygen tank, and had a sleep bypass machine. It was not easy to watch him suffering with so much pain. He was not able to walk from one room to the next without being in pain and out of breath. He was in and out of the hospital a lot. James was a very kind and generous man. He loved feeding people, and was known for smoking the best meat around. He had a big 500 gallon pit on wheels, and would cook whole pigs in it. He was the president of The Owens Park Community Picnic, where he would feed about five hundred people, and he always had enough food. He was dedicated and would work so hard, until I volunteered to help. People came from far and near. The founder of this park was Mrs. Zelma Owens Warren. James would also cook for church events, and he was a great supporter of the church. February 18, 2006 was a special snowy day. James and I ate and watched Bishop T. D. Jakes on DVD. He was explaining how to receive the Lord. This set the stage for me to lead him to the Lord, so I asked him if he wanted to be saved. He said, "Yes" he wanted to receive the Lord. He repeated

Romans 10:9 confessed with his mouth and believed in his heart that Jesus died and rose for his sins, and made Him Lord of his life. On Monday, I went to baby sit the grandchildren after work. It was dark by the time I made it home, and I didn't see James in the house. His breakfast was still on the table, I was wondering why he didn't eat his breakfast. I went to his truck and he was sitting up straight, and had a peaceful look on his face. I felt him breathing, but I couldn't wake him up. I called 911, and then I called Samuel and Lavarange. By the time the ambulance arrived, he was no longer breathing, and later pronounced dead. I was wishing I could have been there with him early. I don't know what happened. A church mother, Mother Noble, said he didn't want me to be there. James has been the only man in my life. It has been over three years since his death. My family truly loved him. We were married 41 years until he died on February 20, 2006.

After my son graduated from high school, he enlisted in the Navy, and was gone for three years. This was very difficult for me, since he was my only son. I will never forget when his clothes where delivered in a brown box. When I saw his shoes; it did something to me inside that I can not even describe. He was alright, but was getting ready to graduate. He had already been through basic training in Waukegan, Illinois. He was then attending school in San Diego, California, for certification as a Fireman Control Technician. His dad and I attended the basic training graduation and the special program the night before the graduation. I remember seeing my son for the first time in two months on that stage singing in the chorus with that priceless smile on his face. He was the only black in his class; I was so proud of him. I was thinking that if only his high school teacher could see him now, she would have been proud also. The next day he marched with the big flag during the graduation ceremony. After Samuel graduated and got out of the Navy, he moved back home and started working different jobs; General Motors, Derden Heating and Cooling Company, and Stuttgart Electric Company, and took a second job at the Pizza Hut. After about five years, he had four children; and became ill. After several tests, he was diagnosed with a kidney disease that resulted in kidney failure. This was a real test of my faith, and it was hard. The more I confessed that he was healed, the sicker he appeared. His body started retaining fluid, and he could not wear his old shoes or pants any longer. I don't know how he kept going, but he did. His blood pressure was high, but he kept going to work at the Pizza Hut. Lavarange and her husband were there for Samuel. One time I kept telling the doctor that God was healing him, so the doctor asked me to leave the room in order for him to talk with Samuel alone. When I was permitted back into the room, the decision had already been made for Samuel to have Dialysis three times a week. This was not easy. He was in and out of the hospital. He kept getting infections, and other complications. I got so many calls from him over the next three years. I was on edge, because James was also sick, and I was the only one to answer every call. One time his heart rate was so high, he told me he thought he was dying, and it was the last time he would see his children. This is still hard for me to share, as I am fighting back the tears. I told him that I believed God was healing him. One day I went to visit my sister, Rose, in Texas. I will always remember this special trip, and the date. On March 7, 2004, we went to the Potter's House, and the guest minister Bishop J. Garlington from California delivered the message. He gave me a prophecy saying, "When you get home tell your son, I can see you in the future, and you look much better than you look right now". This word gave me hope and expectation. I brought the CD, and could hardly wait to give my son the message. As soon as I could call Samuel; I delivered the message, and pinned the words on the wall. I kept it before my eyes and repeated it daily. A year or so later, on April 17, 2005; Samuel called to inform me that he was on his way to Little Rock to get a kidney transplant. Rose was visiting me that week-end, and I had mother also; and we were so excited. We started calling different family members, and everyone was ecstatic and glorifying God. Rose and I went to Little Rock to be with Samuel. Everything was falling into place. He went back for surgery about 6:00 pm and he was back in his room about midnight. He was discharged in four days. He only weighed 127 pounds. He started gaining weight, eating and drinking what he wanted, and his natural color reappeared. Now my baby looks so good, and Bishop Garlington was right, he looks much better now than he did then. He continues working at the Pizza Hut, and also works for Riceland Foods Incorporate as a Rice Bin Distributor. Samuel enjoys working, and also helps at the restaurant. He is married with five children, Quadeja Dejour, LaDarruis Malik, James Samuel, Jr. and Jasmine Shurande (Twins), and Jayden Malachi. I am very proud of him and his family. They are members of my home church. When I was pregnant, the late Elder Clarence Guydon said that I was going to have a boy, and God was going to use him. He also said we should name him Samuel. James wanted to him to have his name, so we named him James Samuel. He has not always been in church, and made good choices. I would remind him of what God said about him. God has truly blessed him and his family, and they recently brought their first house.

I had never been happier for Mother, than seeing her expression when she won that clothes Dryer at the REA meeting. The sad thing about it was that the house burned down before she got a chance to use it. Although they lost everything, no one was injured. George Jr. lived about a mile from us, and he was moving to Stuttgart; so he moved out shortly, leaving the house available for my parents to move in. Dad, Mom, and Andre' stayed with us until the house was ready. People gave everything they needed. The family pictures were missing, so I collected several from family members, and presented them on a DVD as a Christmas present. This was very special, and I am grateful to Nicole, my co-worker's daughter-in-law; for making it happen. Christmas is a big day for our family. We all seen to talk at the same time and listen at the same time. A few years after my parents' house burned down, they bought a house a few blocks from my house. It was good having them so close to me. Dad enjoyed nicknaming the grandchildren; he called Samuel, Iron-head. Samuel loved his Grandma and Papa dearly. I remember Dad had been ill and was diagnosed with prostate cancer. This did not hinder him from driving his four-wheeler in the woods to collect a variety of leaves for Samuel's school assignment.

The doctor informed us the day Dad had surgery that they got all of the cancer and it was not in the limp node. He said he did not need treatments. I sometimes think maybe he did. About two years later, Dad started loosing weight, his color changed, and his eyes changed. May 14, 1991 he went to Stuttgart Hospital for test, and May 21, 1991 he was transported to Baptist Hospital in Little Rock, Arkansas. This is when we were told Dad had lung Cancer, and they started giving him treatments. The doctor assured us that he should be okay. Mother was very upset over this news, and had lost her brother due to Cancer. Dad would go to the hospital regularly for blood and treatments, and he continued to get weaker. He told me to make sure we took care of Mom, because she was forgetting a lot. He wanted to make sure that she was going to be okay. He said if he could live his life over, he would never smoke and never take chemotherapy. I will never forget that day Lavarange called me and said, she was taking Dad to the hospital, and I needed to come. Somehow I knew this was the last time to see my Dad alive. On my arrival to the hospital, I was permitted back where Dad was. I was holding his hand and repeating the 23rd Psalm when I felt his take his last breath. I knew he had gone to be with the Lord, and was not suffering any more. It was exactly 4:30 P.M. on January 21, 1992, and I can still feel this while I am writing. He has been gone for seventeen years, and it does not seem possible. I can still remember hearing the song, "I won't complain" at Dad's the funeral. I thought about how Dad and Mom always did what they could without complaining. They made the best out of whatever they had. Black and white came to show their respect, from far and near. There were so many beautiful flowers with brass flower pots, the funeral home had to make a special trip to bring them to the house, because the church couldn't hold them all. This was a very hard time for Mother, not having Dad there when her mind was diminishing. One of the hardest things I had to do was to take the car keys from her. She would call me repeatedly, because she did not understand. The doctor said she was having mini strokes, so we started keeping her, and rotating turns. I would shop for her, to dress her the way she liked to dress; with matching hats and fine jewelry. She was so pretty and liked pretty colors. I often wondered how one Mother took care of all of us, and it took all of us to take care of one Mother. Earnestine Holt said, "Dewbaby was a remarkable lady, and somebody should put this in a book. She took on seven children at a young age, had just gotten married, and never complained. She treated us like we're her own. She never made a difference". Mother was a faithful worker in the church, and worked on the building fund so we could build our new church. We moved in it in January of this year. We were in the process of building it before she died. She would have been so proud to have seen it.

Mother woke up one Friday morning with a swollen eye, and was taken to the emergency room and admitted in Stuttgart Hospital for tests. Up to that point she was eating and walking. She was given different medications until she continually got worst. After a few weeks, she was transferred to University of Arkansas Medical Center, where she was for over a month, and then released to home hospice care. The medical team kept commenting on how strong she was. She was not expected to live through that month, but she knew we were not ready for her to go. She fought for her life. She moved in with my sister Demetrice. Lavarange moved in with Demetrice to help care for Mother. Mother lived there from January 2006 until her death on May 3, 2007. She was well cared for, and visited by all of her children, the grandchildren, and the great grandchildren; and they loved grandma. I asked, "How can one person give so much in life, and keep giving?" Well, that was my Mom. People came from various states to support us during Mother's Home Going Service. Superintendent Jewell Withers Jr. did the eulogy at both Mother's and Dad's services. He did a wonderful job, and made me realize that she had fought a good fight, and had finished her course. We know to depart and to be with the Lord is far better, and I knew Mother was in good hands. I was thankful that God added another year to her life to help us prepare for her departure, but I guess we would never be ready to say goodbye. My baby brother was having a hard time dealing with Mother's death, but when he saw her in the coffin resting in peace, he said, "She looks gorgeous". I cried more the next Sunday at the Mother' Day Program. I thought about how we took a cake decorating class together, and would bake and decorate cakes for special occasions. My pastor, Elder Jeffery said I was receiving Mother's spirit; then I understood. My sister, Rose, wanted us to start a restaurant for many years, and to write a book. Well, after Mother passed, we opened the Restaurant in her honor. We named it, "Dew-Baby's Restaurant". I bake the desserts and make the cornbread dressing weekly. I cook a lot like Mother, and my sisters are good cooks. We have a lot of fun working together. Mother showed us how to love.

My name is Betty Louise (Jeffery) Watkins

I am the sixth child of George and Giristine Jeffery. I was born June 30, 1947, in the community of Almyra, Arkansas. Mother said she was eight months pregnant with me when her mother died. Therefore, I never got a chance to meet my grandmothers because my father's mother had died also. I never knew my mother's father, however; I did know my daddy's father, and I loved my grandpa Ed. My cousin Cleo lived with my grandpa, and we were in the same grade in school. Therefore; I would spend nights with my grandpa when we were taking school trips. Cleo would look out for me like a big brother. We lived in the woods and my grandpa lived on the highway, so the bus would pick us up at grandpa's house.

Since I was a very young child, I have had a desire to know God. When I learned how to read, reading my Bible was a priority. The Bible always fascinated me; I loved reading Bible stories and playing Church. I would gather my congregation of brothers and sisters and read the Bible stories to them. I became a Christian at the age of twelve years old. Church has always been a vital part of my life, even when we did not have transportation we walked six miles to and from Church, up and down a dirt road. I could not get to Church fast enough, when I would hear the congregation singing I would start to run, because I did not want to miss anything. Once I got inside it was worth every mile I had walked.

I went to Immanuel Elementary School, in a small rural community of Almyra, Arkansas. We lived so far back in the woods we had to walk a mile to catch the school bus. Our bus stop was at a grocery store, but we had no money to shop at this store. I remember many days looking at the candy, cookies, and all the other goodies; and saying to myself that one day I am going to grow up and buy all the goodies I want. The Mitchell's, the store owners were very nice people, and would sometimes give us some goodies because they knew we could not afford them. However; our parents taught us not to take anything that did not belong to us because that is stealing, and if we were caught stealing; we would have to answer to mom and dad, and no goodies were worth that. We also had a nice bus driver, Mr. Saul Dunn, who some times would go in the grocery store and buy us goodies. Mom and Dad made sure we were fed and had plenty of food to eat, so we were not hungry. However; the candies and cookies were different from the food we had. Our food came from the garden, lakes, and the woods. Mom was a great gardener, and dad was a very good fisherman and hunter. I remember many nights hurrying to bed before dad got home with all those fish to clean. He always knew we were not asleep and were trying to avoid cleaning the fish. He would come to the bedroom door, and politely say, "Those fish better be cleaned tonight". We would get out of the bed running to clean those fish. Dad was a man of a few words, but they were very powerful words. Many times my school lunch was the game dad brought back from hunting, or from the crop we raised. Many times I would eat my lunch before we got to school, because I was embarrassed of what I had to eat. Sometimes I would eat my lunch on break behind the hedges. One day I had baked sweet potatoes. I was rushing and eating them, I heard someone coming, so I swallowed the whole potato and almost choked. On another occasion, our bus was late arriving at the school because it had mechanical troubles. My sister, Lavarange, and I were debating who would carry the lunch pail to the classroom. Our classrooms were all in one building, with a long hall between them. We had peanuts in the lunch pail, and we were both embarrassed. We were already late, so I grabbed the lunch pail and rushed down the hall. I guess I was in too big of a hurry, because I tripped and fell and all those peanuts spilled out and were rolling down the hall and into the classrooms. There I lay in the middle of our lunch on the floor, and looking up at all those students laughing at me. They were laughing so hard the teachers could not control them. I was so embarrassed. I did not want to go to class.

I was a very shy and tenderhearted person. I was also a person of few words, like Dad. I remember the first time I was asked to make a presentation in front of the class, I was so nervous my knees were weak and knocking together, and my lips were trembling. I studied hard to learn my lessons and eventually was an honor student. I sang in the school choir and I enjoyed singing. I was very athletic. I represented our school in competition with other schools. During the field days, other schools would come to our school to compete with us in jumping, running, and other sports. I was such a high jumper until one day I frighten myself, I jumped as high as a house, and Lavarange witnessed it. I represented in all of the races and I always won 1ˢᵗ place. Maybe this was my spot for the Olympics. Could I have missed my calling?

Dad was a farmer. We missed school days when harvest time came to work in the fields. We were permitted to attend school during testing times. Our cotton fields were located on the bus route, and if we were in the fields when the bus passed by the children would make fun of us. I would be so embarrassed that I would duck down trying to hide, but I couldn't.

As a teenager, I worked in a private home for Dr. and Mrs. Eldridge. They were very nice to me. I worked my way through high school. Mrs. Eldridge made my graduation dress for our class night. It was gorgeous; it had three layers of lace on the tale, underneath was an attached lining, a slip with three layers of ruffles, and beautiful satin bows all around the lace. I knew I was the best dressed person in the whole class. My class was the last class to graduate from this school and the school closed in 1965. I never will forget the day I received the tragic news that Mrs.

Eldridge's was killed in an accident on the tractor. Although she was a classy lady, they also were farmers. She did not mind getting dirty. Even now it is hard for me to talk about her death.

After graduation I moved to Clarendon, Arkansas, and lived with my sister, Demetrice and her husband. She has always been my mentor, and to me she could do no wrong. I have always admired her and think that she is a beautiful person inside and out. I admired her relationship with God and how she stood for what was right even if it hurts. She was so smart and informative, and loved learning. I recall as a child her being the first person to wake up during the cool winter to make a fire in the potbelly wood burning stove. When we got up it was already hot. I worked for Sharks and Tarzan Television factory for two years. Then I got the disappointing news that the plant was closing and moving over seas. I was contemplating moving to Detroit, Michigan until a close friend advised me otherwise, and I am glad I listened.

I moved to the big city, Little Rock, Arkansas. Then I was on my own and I had a full load. I was attending Opportunity Industrial Center School at night, working at Timex watch factory at night, and working at the Dairy Queen on week-ends. I received a Certificate in Clerk Typing, and Upholstery. Then Dad came and surprised me, he asked me if I could handle a car. I was so excited, I replied, "Yes Dad I can handle it". So Dad helped me purchase my first car, and it was a white Ford Falcon. I named it "Rickasha". After I got the car, I let it remain parked for a long time, because I was afraid to drive in the city. Although I had a car, I was still riding on the street bus to work. One day I was faced with a real dilemma, I had an appointment that was not in the bus schedule. I had to make a decision to miss my appointment or to drive. Well, I prayed and decided to drive. Once I got on the road I realized that it was not as bad as I had imagined. I have been driving every since that day.

I continued to be active in church. I received my Missionary license from the Church of God in Christ. I conducted revival services, as well as speaking engagements. While minding my own business and taking care of God's business, I was attracted to a young man, Minister Archie

Grant. I loved his spirit; he was very active in church, friendly, and caring. He said whatever he wanted to say, and began to pursue me. He had told my sisters that he was going to marry me before he asked me. We got married on October 20, 1969. We were supposed to have gotten married October 18, 1969. We both went to the courthouse at the agreed time, but we were on opposite ends, and we could not find each other. This was before cell phones came out, so we had no means of communicating; and we both were frustrated. In fact, he was so upset and determined not to leave without the marriage license, they had to call the police to calm him down. So this set our wedding date back, and we had to wait until Monday. This really messed things up, because I had left my car in Stuttgart, so we could ride back together. Therefore, on our wedding night my husband and I both had to drive back to Little Rock. I was in my wedding gown trailing my husband to Little Rock.

My husband was a good person and he had such compassion for people. One evening he called me to pick him up from work, but I knew he drove his car to work so I asked him what is wrong with your car. He replied, "Well Brother White has a large family and he needed a car, so I gave him my car". He was too generous at times, however; God always blessed us. He was a Vietnam Veteran, and at times he would have temper flair ups, but they did not last long, and he would be so apologetic afterwards. I never doubted his love for me; everyone knew that he loved Betty. He worked for Harold Hall Roofing Company, and loved his job. On August 16, 1977, I was at work in the office of GTE, and two men came to my desk and asked me, "Are you Betty Grant?", and I replied, "Yes". They asked if we could meet for a moment, and I said, "Sure". One of them said, "Well, I am sorry, Archie just got electrocuted on the job". I nearly passed out, and I was trembling and screaming; this was like something I could not believe. I had to be taken to the hospital for medication to calm me down. It was very hard for me to deal with. I could not go back to the house for a week. This was a pain that I could not explain, for many weeks. Eventually God lifted the burden. I had said that I would never marry again. I finally moved back to the mobile house we bought together after Rose, Deborah, and a friend, Creola, moved in with me. In January 1978, my mobile home burned and we had to move and split up. I then decided to build a house. What an experience that was. After all of the decisions for the house, we finally moved back together in a new house. We all furnished our own rooms and were sharing the house note since we were all single, it was working out good. Well all three of the girls got married within 6 months and leaving me home alone. Now this was a real challenge, but I kept working in the church and the district. I was the Youth chairlady of the district and I loved working with the youth.

When I was in the 9th grade, Jewell, Lavarange, and I rode the Grey Hound Bus to Detroit, Michigan, to visit my mother's aunt and cousins. Our cousin, Ethel, was in a convalescent home. She was obese with other health problems. She was so sweet. This was an exciting trip to go to the big city. We went over to Canada, and had a choice to go through a tunnel or on a long bridge. I was not fond of either route, but we ended up going one way and coming back the other way. I remember Canada being a very clean place. I thought the people were talking funny, and they were asking us where we were from. When we told them that we were from Stuttgart, they thought we were from Stuttgart, Germany. That was the last time I traveled to Detroit with Lavarange, because she got married before me, and I was older. This affected me, because I thought I should have gotten married before Lavanage. I cried so hard at her wedding and it felt like I was loosing my best friend. People were consoling me by telling me that somebody wanted me, but that was not it at all.

We were in revival at my home church in Casscoe, Arkansas, conducted by a renowned Evangelist, Alfred Hinton. This was a powerful revival. My pastor, Elder Clarence Guydon invited his cousin from Kansas City, to the revival to meet the Evangelist. When I met him I knew he was my husband. However, I did not tell him what I knew. He told me that God told him I was his wife. The first night

I shook his hand there was such a connection that knocked him back against the wall. Of course, he will deny it. We communicated over the telephone long hours and he made lots of unexpected visits. My friend, Cathy Robinson, would invite us out to dinner just to watch us look at each other. We were so in love. He was the kindest, most romantic man I had ever met. I felt like a Queen when I was with him. To make a long story short, we were married in 6 months, on September 13, 1980. He was a pastor in Kansas and he closed the ministry to move to Almyra, Arkansas. We were the pastors of a church in Dewitt, Arkansas, for many years. Then my husband said he felt the leading of the Lord to start an independent ministry. We started this ministry in Dewitt, Arkansas and it also closed. We then attended a church in Little Rock for about three years. Then my husband said he was ready to begin another church. I did not want to hear anything about pastoral ministry again. However, I prayed and got in submission to what he thought was God's will. We started back in pastoral ministry in 1990 in Little Rock, Arkansas. My husband became a bishop and a doctor of divinity. Things were progressing in the ministry. We had a good outreach, feeding the disadvantaged, a Bible school, and we had fellowship churches under our ministry. We even opened up our home to people. God was really blessing us. After years of working in the ministry, and loving God's people; I was betrayed by my husband. This ended the ministry and the marriage. This was no easy test of my faith in God. I went through a period of grieving the loss of both, but God held my hand throughout the entire process. I am still in contact with some of the former members because my love for them has not changed my committed to praying that they stay in the faith. I pray that they remain strong in the Lord and in the power of His might, and that they be not entangled again with the yoke of bondage. No matter what comes our way, God has already designed our escape. He is faithful to His Word, so it does not matter who leaves you, or what you have left. Be content with what you have, for He has said, "I WILL NEVER LEAVE THEE, NOR FORSAKE THEE. So that we may boldly say, THE LORD *IS* MY HELPER, AND I WILL NOT FEAR WHAT

MAN SHALL DO UNTO ME." (Hebrews 13:5, 6) God doesn't need what you've loss to fulfill His purpose in your life. He can shut doors that no man can open, and open doors that no man can shut.

I am happy to report that God has blessed me with another preacher. He is a former pastor and he is no stranger. His Dad was my District superintendent over thirty years ago. It is so amazing how God works things out, and I love it. Yes, I am happily married to Jonathan Watkins. God is faithful.

Lavarange Davis

I am the 7th child, born November 2, 1948, in Casscoe, Arkansas. We are a very close knit family. We all live close together. Rose is the only sister living out of state, in Texas. I live about three blocks from where I was raised. Even after getting married, I did not move far away. A few years later, I came right back down here with my husband. The old proverb says, "You can take the person out of the country, but you can't take the country out of the person". I am a living witness of that, and "apples don't fall far from the tree". Mom told me I was undeveloped as a baby, and the doctor prescribed vitamins to enhance my growth. I think those vitamins had steroids in them, because they grew my legs so long, mom said they were hanging out of the baby bed. Needless to say, I am the tallest girl in the family and I'll give the boys a run for their money. I am 6 feet tall, and I cover all the ground I stand on. I still had developmental delays in my motor skills. I was 15 months old when I started walking. My family did everything they knew to teach me how to walk, and it didn't work. Mom said that she prayed for me, and one day I just got down from the sofa and walked across the floor. Mom said, "Praise God, my baby can walk". Mom planted the seed in my life that I am blessed and highly favored of the Lord because I am the 7th child.

We had our challenges, but our parents made everything alright. Betty and I were very close coming up. We did so many things together. One day we decided that we were going to get all the briar rabbit syrup we wanted, so we took the ½ gallon bucket of syrup with two biscuits and hid behind the house. We ate the whole ½ gallon bucket of syrup, and we were as sick as a dog. We kept running to the bathroom. Earnestine, called "Totsie" told Betty that she had Diarrhea, and she started crying and crying. Mom asked her what was she crying about, and she said, "Tostie said we are going to die for real". Mom then explained to us what she meant. She did not whip us; she did not have to, because the syrup did that. We practically stayed in the bathroom for three days. Mom gave us pepto bismol, floured water; and that did the trick. We learned a valuable lesson, that mom knew more than we did. And she never had any more problems with us eating too much syrup.

I don't remember my other sisters getting into as much trouble as I did. One day I threw a brick at Betty and she ducked, and it hit the headlight on Dad's car. That was the first and last time Dad had to discipline me.

I think Mom was one of the world's best cooks. She could make a meal out of just about anything. She didn't have to measure anything. She would put a little of this and a little of that and it became a perfect meal. The tea cakes were so good that I could never get enough. One night when I thought everyone was asleep, I sneaked into the kitchen to get another tea cake. I knew where mom kept them; in the flour barrel behind the cooking stove. Just as soon as I lifted myself over in the barrel, dad pushed me in. I was crying, and he was laughing at me with flour all over my face. Mom came in, and after she saw my face looking like a ghost; she said, "George, let that girl up out of there". I still didn't get a whipping, but I didn't do that again. My parents had a lot of love and care for all of us. When things got tough, seemingly our parents got tougher. I am sure they would reflect back and wonder how they made it, but they put their trust in the Lord. We had food to eat and to share, we had clothes to wear, water to drink, and a roof over our heads.

Family

Dad required us to kiss him on the jaw before he gave us candy, but my sister Lillie never would. I had no problems getting my candy and would have gotten Lillie's if I could. Our parents worked together, and were not passive in raising us. I am glad that they didn't let me do everything my little mind led me to do, because there is no telling what I would have ended up doing, or being.

I remember Dad building a table with chairs big enough to seat all of us. He also built a play ground. I still feel like we were the most blessed children in the world to have had such wonderful parents. Mom was a very clean person and believed in us being clean. Many times we would catch the rain outside in tubs, and use water from the pump. We got heavy snow, sometimes 10 inches, and mom would use it to make ice cream. I really miss that. We created our own games like little sally walker, marbles, mud cakes, and etc. We played outside at night and God protected us.

We were the first black family in our community to get electricity and to own a black and white television. That was in the early 50's, and the neighborhood children would come and watch TV with us. We would watch programs like Cheyenne Boodie, Wolf man, Frank-N-Stine, Boss and Blacke, Sugar foot, and others. We only had two channels, 11 and 7, but that was good enough for us. We would pop a huge pan full of popcorn. We enjoyed sharing because our parents trained us to share, and to do unto others as we wanted them to do unto us.

The name of our light company was R.E.A. They held annual meetings and would giveaway a gift. I attended a meeting with Mom and the host asked everyone who had over 3 children to stand, and then he said if you have more than 5 children remain standing, each time they increase the number there were people taking their seat. He continued and said if you have more than 7 children remain standing, and then more than 9, then 11, then 13; and Mom was the only one left standing. Finally, he asked, lady how many children do you have? Mom won a clothes dryer, and she was ecstatic. The entire family was so excited, because we had worked for everything we had; and to win something, it was like unreal. We could now dry clothes inside for the first time. This was one of God's special blessings.

Although we did not have everything some of my friends had, we had the most important things like love and values.

I will never forget when my little brothers, Fredrick and Larry, stole Dad's traps, and set them in the wrong place. When Dad came home, he told them to go and get his traps. When they got to the place where they left the traps, a skunk was caught by the feet. When they approached their prey, he defended himself aggressively. Although they did not bring their prey home, it was no doubt what they caught. Mom made them sit outside, and bathe in tomato juice, but it didn't work. That ended their trap stealing career, and they later found out that Dad saw the skunk in the trap on the way home.

I am so thankful that God hears a child's prayer. I experienced this for myself when I had a few boils on my body. They were so painful that I could not stand for mom to touch them. My oldest sister, Jewell, took me to the doctor, and he had to ask Jewell to help hold me on the table. As the doctor was lancing and squeezing out the infection, Jewell was assisting him in restraining me. I was crying, screaming, and kicking. The next day, my right arm was swollen, I could not straighten it out, and it was another boil.

Mom said I would have to go back to the doctor if it did not go away in a couple of days.

I prayed and ask God to please let it go away. I didn't want to see that doctor anymore.

Two days later, I was walking to the store and was chased by a dog. I run so fast that I tripped and fell on my arm. When I got home, Mom noticed that I had burst the boil, and she managed to clean it and squeeze the infection out of it. God answered my prayer and to this day I have never had another boil. I thank God that He is concerned about us.

I could pick over 400 pounds of cotton a day in temperatures over 100 degrees. I made $2.50 per 100 pounds. Although we missed a lot of school days working the fields, we all graduated from High school, and several graduated from college or trade school. I went to Phillips Community College and studied nursing, but I did not graduate. I did work as a nurse's aide and became an emergency medical technician (EMT). When I was a child, I put dirt on my sister's foot to stop the bleeding after she cut herself. Taking care of people has been my passion.

Mom was diagnosed with Alzheimer, and died from an Aneurism in her stomach May 3, 2007. I was with her the entire time. During the last years of Mom's life, Demetrice and I took care of her. I thought about all the years she took care of us, and this compelled me to go the extra mile to make her as comfortable as possible. Although it required commitment, this was one of the most meaningful periods of my life. She would bring joy, and made us laugh many times. My relief comes from knowing that she is with the Lord, in whom she loved so much. Mother was a singer and enjoyed singing praise songs. Even when we could not understand her words much in her final stages, she would sing along with us and move to praise songs. It really saddens my heart to see children not engaged in any way with their senior feeble parents. We should not despise them when they are old, because if we keep living our day is coming. Mom always told us, what goes around comes around. It is much too easy to get caught up in the conveniences God have blessed us with, and not wanting to inconvenienced ourselves to help others. I can't forget the sacrifice Jesus made for us. He left all his convenience, made Himself a servant, and gave His life. He said, I was sick and you did not come to see about me. (Matthew 25:43)

In my senior year of school I transferred to Holman High school, Stuttgart, Arkansas. This was due to integration; we rode the bus with the white children. They were not nice to us. They called us, "niggers" and threw spit balls at us. A few of them knew us well, but they didn't say a word and the bus drive didn't say a word. This made us afraid to ride the bus, so we prayed, and those people became our friends.

I graduated May 19, 1967. I said that my dream was to get married. I was dating Joe Lewis Davis and he had not yet proposed to me. Shortly after I graduated, he proposed to me. He was a deacon in his church and a good man. I did not want him to ask Mom. I told him to ask Dad if he could marry me, and Dad's response was, "whatever Mom said will be alright with me". Mom explained that I had just graduated, and I didn't know what I wanted to do yet; but Deacon Joe didn't stop until he got permission. We got married June 18, 1967, and were married for 37 years until his death December 2, 2004.

I called him "Honey", and he was sweet to me. He never missed a special occasion, doing something special for me. We would go out to eat often go and on trips. Once we went to Detroit, I lost my wedding ring. He just bought me another one. He was my best friend. In our early years, we went through some things, because he had backslidden. I had to deal with unfaithfulness, and other things. We dealt with it, maybe not in the best way, but thank God for grace. We survived! I thank God for I John 1:9 "If we confess our sins, He is faithful and just to forgive us and to cleanse us from all unrighteousness". Because I was young when I got married, I had to learn that marriage is not about one becoming his or her own person. It is about two people becoming one according to Matthew 19:6. We did not have any children together, but Honey had a son before we got married, Joe Jr. God brought him back. Honey testified how my sister, Rose, kept showing him love and inviting him back to church. Honey was an example to me how Christ loved the church, because he loved me unconditionally, and was so self sacrificing. We prayed together, and that was one of the keys to the success in our marriage. We played a lot and had so much fun. Honey was such a compassionate man. I would bring so many homeless and distressed people home with me, and Honey would let them stay with us until they got themselves on their feet. We would study the Bible with them and take them to church with us. They would tell us that it is so peaceful out here. They can think clearly. People would ask us how we had such a great marriage. We respected each other, and we looked out for the best interest of each other. We had our challenges, but you were willing to work things out. I believe in praying and asking God for a mate. I tell women to let the man find them. It worked for me, and I was married to one man for 37 years. God knows what we need more than we can image. If you put your trust in Him, he will show you ways you will never figure out on you own. I am a witness that it does not matter how you start out, but how you finish. Always reach for the highest things in life, and set your affections on things above. Then God will take you to a place where man can't ever take you. Honey was called into the ministry after we got married. He became the Evangelist president of our church district, and eventually the pastor of my home church, Mt. Calvary COGIC the last three years of his life. He retired from Riceland Foods as an Extractor operator for 30 years. I've always had a caring heart for people, and I worked at The Crest Park Nursing Home for two years. In 1969, I worked for Stuttgart Memorial Hospital for 17 years, and then for 20 years I did private sitting.

One night I came home, when I got to the door and got ready to put the key into the door, I heard a snort. I looked around and saw a bear in the yard. I was so nervous, I was shaking. I managed to get the key in the door and went in the house. I started calling Demetrice and it was hard for me to dial the phone. I had to use one hand to stabilize the other hand, in order to dial the phone. When I finally got my sister on the phone, I was barely moving my mouth and Demetrice kept saying, "Who is this, I can't hear you". In fear that she would hang up, I said with all my might, "Dee, it's a bear". Then she said, "It's not in the house, is it?" I said, "No", and she said, "Well, stay in the house". When I hung up, I called Larry, and I told him about the bear, and he came and drove around. When Honey got home, I opened the door and flagged for him not to get out of the car, but he did not understand and he got out of the car. I then told him that I saw a bear, and he told me to get back in the house, and he got back in the car. He drove around, and then came in the house. Larry called later and said he saw him running towards the woods.

Honey was very devoted to his work at Riceland Foods, and almost had a 30 year perfect attendance record, until he fell off a 20 foot scaffold at work and injured himself. Before the fall, he was never under the doctor's care. He was in good health and had no physical complaints. After the fall, he suffered many complications, and was prescribed different medications. He had worked all of his life and he tried to keep going to work. He was put on light duty for a while, but it was too painful for him to continue, so he retired (involuntarily). This took a lot out of him, but he said that he gave it all to the Lord.

On Wednesday night December 1, 2004, we went to mid week service at church. Many of the church members were teasing him about how dressed up he was. When we got home I asked him if he wanted anything to eat. He said, "Yes". He ate one bite and said it was good, but that was all he wanted. I told him that I was going to save it for his breakfast, but he said that he would not be eating breakfast. He kept looking at me, and said that he loved me. I told him that I loved him too, and he said that he knew that I did. I told him that I knew he was not trying to go to bed without me, and I would be on. He replied that I was going to fall asleep on the couch, and wake up at 3:00 AM. Then he said, "You will be alright". He went to bed, and when I woke up it was 3:00 AM; and I said, "That man, he said that I would do this". I got in the bed and shook him, but he did not move. I then turned the light on, and he was not breathing. I kept saying, "Honey, please don't do this to me". I did CPR trying to resuscitate him, and nothing worked. I called 911, and they recognized me, because I formerly worked with them. The person on the phone tried to calm me down, and told me to continue doing the CPR and they were on their way. He asked me if anyone lived close, and I told him that Demetrice and Larry lived close to me; and he told me to call them and he would call right back. So I called them, and they came right away. Larry assisted me doing the CPR, until the ambulance arrived. He was not receiving any air; and seeing them drive off with him after 37 years was more than I could express. He took such good care of me, and now I could not do anything for him. I didn't get to say goodbye. I wondered did he know, because God would reveal things to Him. He was a prophet, and Amos 3:3 says, "God will not do anything unless He first revealed it to His servant the prophets". He was a praying man, faithful to the work of God, and loved people. The one thing I would say to wives is not to wait until it is so late to tell your mate how much he means to you, because when that opportunity is taken away, it is very painful. Only God gave me the strength and comfort I needed to continue without him. I don't know how I would have made it without Him. I found hope in knowing that I was left here for a purpose, and I seek to fulfill that purpose. I ended up moving in with my sister, Demetrice, down the road from me. It was difficult for me to live in the same house again. I could still hear Momma saying, "Gal, you can't pay that no attention, you have to trust God".

Lillie Mae Jeffery

I was born May 11, 1950 to the parents of George and Girstine Jeffery. I am number eight of the fourteen children. My parents made great sacrifices for us, as well as   assuming the responsibility of raising seven extended family members.   That shows how much they valued families staying together, and sharing with one another. They were a young married couple, and teenagers, producing a family themselves. They did not want to see extended family members sent to a foster home, put up for adoption, or split among different family members. So, in order to guarantee that the Holt family would stay together and be loved; my parents raised them along with us. I thank God for my parents who loved enough to extend beyond their fourteen children to another family. In deed that's the God kind of love. Only God can give one the capacity to love like that, and beyond your own family.

I remember Mother having her big Bible on the coffee table and she would open it up and read it, seemly everyday. We were raised up in Church. Mother would carry us to Church every service. We knew how to conduct ourselves, and if we misbehaved in Church; all Mother would do is give us that look, and we got back in line. We wanted to talk to our friends sometimes, while the adults were into the service; but we quickly learned that was the wrong time.

Mother would always invite the preacher and his family over for Sunday dinner. She would let them eat first, and sometimes they would eat up everything she cooked. She never complained; she just cooked another meal so we could eat. The Sunday meal was a special event for Mother. She would start preparing on Saturday night, and the aroma would go through the house. Mother was a great cook. When we smelled the food cooking, we could almost taste it, and could hardly wait to eat. I remember one particular Saturday night; Mother had prepared Sunday's dinner and put it up. We could still smell the meatloaf, although she warned us to leave it alone. Shortly after that, my brother George Jr., called "Joe" decided to get a piece anyway. I walked in the kitchen and caught him in the act. When I saw him putting a piece of meatloaf in his mouth, and chewing it; I threatened to tell Mother. He tried hard to convince me that it wasn't him that I saw, that it was his twin brother; but there is no twin. You would have to know my brother Joe, to understand that he would try to con his way out of anything. I then asked him, "What is that I see all over your mouth?" Well, he must be a pro, because he paid me off with two quarters, not to tell it. That was a lot of money to me, so I didn't tell it. When Mother asked who got in the meatloaf? I said, "I don't know, but it sure wasn't Joe". I had no intentions of giving up my money.

Our family' garden was the source of most of our food. Mother would can food, and put food in the freezer for the winter months. My Daddy was a fisherman, and I believed he went fishing nearly everyday. Mother made sure we had a well balanced meal. I remember eating oatmeal and homemade biscuits every morning. I did not eat greens, so she would cook beans every evening just for me. She also made homemade dessert every day. She put a lot of love and care into every meal, and you could taste the difference. She was known for making big tea cakes. I regret no one got the recipe from her. I have tasted many others, but I have never tasted another one like the ones she made. She made sure we all ate breakfast before we went to school. She said that it is the most important meal of the day. Then she would always fix our lunch bucket, and that is just what it was, a (Johnnie Fair) bucket full of lunch. Sometimes we would walk off and intently leave it, because we were ashamed of what she had fixed (biscuits and peanut butter sandwiches, baked sweet potatoes, and peanuts). When Mother would see that we left our lunch bucket, she would chase the bus down to give us our lunch. Although we would tell the bus driver to speed up, Mother would be faster.

Mother was always busy, and she did not believe in wasting anything. I remember her making our slips out of flour cotton sacks. I was careful to keep my clothes nice. My sister Lavarange was very mischievous; she would ask me if she could wear an outfit of mine to school, I would tell her no because she did not take care of her clothes. She would wait until I lift the house, and than she would come stepping out with my outfit on. She knew how to aggravate me. She was always getting into stuff, but she has a caring heart. She would stay up all night and fan us with a hand fan in the summers.

Daddy was a hard working farmer. The main crop that we had to work was the cotton. I remember getting home from school. As soon as the bus arrived, the first thing I would see was cotton sacks lined up on the ground. Daddy had laid them out for us to go and pick cotton. He did not need to hire any help, because he had enough children to take care of the corps, we could really pick cotton. I remember the first time I picked 100 pounds of cotton; Daddy gave me 50 cent. I thought I was rich, but I later found out I had a long ways to go. I eventually was able to pick more cotton, and picked over 300 pounds a day. You understand why Dad didn't need any hired help in the cotton fields. Most of my sisters could pick from 300 to 400 pounds per day. We kept Daddy going to the cotton gin to empty the load.

I attended Immanuel School in Almyra, Arkansas from the first grade to the tenth grade. We had prayer every day at school. My teachers displayed love and patience. We were like one big family home away from home school. The teachers were like our parents, they did not spare the rod. If we acted up in school, we would get disciplined and when we got home, we would get disciplined again. In 1966, Immanuel High School closed its' doors. I was in the tenth grade, and this was an emotional time for our family school. I was going to the eleventh grade to a new environment, and a new school. I was faced with many uncertainties. How is this new school? How are the teachers? What about my friends? Where the lessons the same? I transferred to Holman High School in Stuttgart, Arkansas. Some of my classmates went to a different school. This new school was not bad. I graduated with honors in May 1968.

My first secular employment was at Kroger Store in Stuttgart, Arkansas in 1970. A few years ago, that store closed and I was transferred to another Kroger Store in DeWitt, Arkansas. After 39 years, I am still employed for Kroger. I love my job. It is one of the avenues that God is using to be a blessing to the family, the Church, and others. I have worked for Kroger so long; that I have had the opportunity to work in every department of the operation. I remember when I first started; the "N" word was used very loosely. The customers would say things like, "I don't want that Nigger checking me out". I would go home and cry every night. I started thinking that I could not continue to work under those circumstances. First of all, the store was boycotted in order to employ Blacks; and I was one of the first Blacks hired. I endured that season of discomfort, and God has brought me through victorious. Thirty nine years has gone by, and now I am one of the best employees in the company. I am not bragging, but I do my job very well. I also work very hard at our restaurant, "Dew-Baby's". We went on our first cruise to Jamaica and the Cayman Islands this year.

I married at the age of 18 years old. We lived in Detroit during that first year, and later moved back home. During the later years of the marriage, he started using drugs, and only God kept my mind and me safe. One day he came to my job and picked me up. He viciously attacked me, pushing me out of the rolling car, and took me to the dam to throw me in. Only God's grace and mercy spared my life. He had lifted my body, to throw me in the dam, and then God intervened and made him sick. He put me down on the ground, started vomiting, put me back in the car, and then he drove me to Stuttgart Hospital to get medical treatment for my injuries. Thank God my sister-in-law, Bessie

Jeffery was working there; it was good to see a family member in a time like that. After examination, I was taken to Little Rock for further treatment. Before I left Stuttgart Hospital, Mother and Lavarange were right by my side. I stayed with my parents during my recovery. We then divorced in 1981. We were married for 13 years with no children. My sister, Rose, witnessed to him, and he started going to church. I pray that he made peace with God.

I married Bill Arnold in 1982. We have two children, Charity Arnold and Caleb Arnold; and one granddaughter, Azaria Kamil Austin. Bill and I were divorced this year, due to years of abandonment.

I am a member of Progressive Church in Scott, Arkansas. Pastor Syvaster VanBurean II is the Pastor. We are taught to live the Word of God, and to have faith in God. I work in the kitchen ministry, where we feed 25 to 40 people every Sunday. This is an enjoyable experience, and I am doing what God has gifted me to do. My Church is very supportive, and is a lot like my biological family; with enough love to expand to others.

The Biography of Deborah (Jeffery) Brown

I am Deborah, the 9th child. Dad was 19 years old when he married Mom, and she was 18 years old. They married in 1938. To this union was born 14 single births, I and my 13 siblings. Dad was born August 29, 1919. He was born in Arkansas County, Keaton Township. Dad died on January 21, 1992. Mom was born April 11, 1920, in Arkansas County. Mom died May 3, 2007.

The order of my siblings are: my oldest sister, Jewell was born October 14, 1939; Juanita was born on November 5, 1941; Demetrice was born on April 7, 1943; my oldest brother, George, Jr. was born October 9, 1944; Mary Ann was born on September 19, 1945; Betty was born on Jun 30, 1947; Lavarange was born on November 2, 1948; Lillie Mae was born May 11, 1950; Of course, I'm here, born July 29, 1952; then another brother, Frederick was born on July 11, 1953; Rose Mary was born October 4, 1954; Larry was born July 25, 1956; Glenda was born December 19, 1959; and last but not least, Andre' Lozar was born January 27, 1966. Now there you have it ... One BIG HAPPY Family! But wait; there is something else you should know about my family. Mom and Dad became the legal guardians over seven Holt siblings, after they had been married about two years when they undertook this huge responsibility. The love they both had for children and family stood the test. To avoid splitting up the Holt's siblings, after the loss of their parents, grandparents, and aunts; they took them in. There were four girls and three boys. At the time Mom and Dad accepted them, their ages ranged from two years old to fourteen years old. Arthur was the oldest of the Holts and Letha Mae was the youngest. The others in between were Freddie, Willie Lee, Earnestine, Rosie Lee, and Hattie. Earnestine never got married, and she remained at home with the family during the time I was born and throughout my childhood. She took me under her wings when my brother, Frederick, was born. I grew so close to Earnestine, better known as "Totsie". I convinced myself that Totsie was my Mom. Just a little hint on how the older siblings stepped up to the plate and helped around the house with the younger siblings when the other children were born, it was incredible. However, the real Mom did not take this for granted. She immediately recognized each child's need, and was there to provide the love and attention that we needed. Needless to say, Mom knew what was in my head and assured me that she was the Mom and that it was okay to love Totsie, but as a sister.

There was never a dull moment around our house, and that is for sure. The family grew into a close knitted family with lots of love and excitement.

During my childhood we played outside, in the woods, and down the road almost all day long. Arthur and Rosie Lee lived just down the road from us. We grew up with their children and they were great playmates. We swung on tree limbs, ropes from trees, rode bicycles, rolled barrels down the dusty roads, played in the high grass, and explored the great outside. The exercise was good for us. We were certainly healthy and physically fit. When I was a little girl, my favorite outside sport was to jump rope. My sister, Rose, and Arthur's daughters, (Wilma and Winnie) and I would play hot peas. Though we probably invented the hot pea's level of rope jumping, we were really good at it. I became so strong in my legs and swift on my feet, and this continued throughout my school age years. I was very good in physical education and was even awarded with a gymnastic gold metal on class night in May 1970.

It's so funny reminiscing on the past. My first day of school was a day I will never forget. Mom got me all dressed up and watched me hold hands with my older sister, Betty, as that "Big-Old" yellow bus pulled up and off we went. The closer we got the campus of Immanuel School, the sicker my stomach felt. Betty made sure I was placed in the correct classroom with Mrs. Myrtle Montgomery. Before Betty could get out the door, I was right on her trail clinging to her begging her not to leave me. Betty turned and took me back and explained to me that I had to stay with my class and she needed to go to her class. This process went on most of the day. Finally, Mrs. Myrtle had enough of me being spoiled and decided to break the cycle. She just picked me up and told Betty to go ahead to her class. Then she sat me down right beside her, and told me I was not going with Betty so stop crying because we had lots of work to do. She said we were going to have fun doing it. At this point, I was kind of in a state of shock, but I loved school from that moment on. Thanks to that little old teacher, Ms. Myrtle Montgomery, I ended up being very studious and remained an honor student throughout school. I graduated from high school in the top ten of my class.

When I was born, Mom and Dad only had one son and I was the eighth daughter. Totsie named me "Deborah", after the judge in the Bible. The next child born was a boy, and so on; it was a girl, then boy, then girl, and finally boy.

When we were growing up, unlike children today, we ate what was put before us. There were no options to be picky eaters. Mom knew if we absolutely did not like a certain type of food, in that case she would substitute our meal. However, we were required to at least taste the dish before we announced, "I don't like it". We could not just look at the food and not taste it, but had to engage our taste buds. We were blessed to have cooked meals every day. We were not allowed to play with the food or to waste food.

I use to make and save many different objects with pop-sickle sticks. These were dear to me, but my collection treasury did not with-stand the house fire our family experienced in 1968. I was fifteen years old when we lost everything in the house fire, but we were very grateful that we all were spared and we still had each other.

My parents were incredible. As a child I never even dreamed of doing foolish things behind their backs, because my oldest brother, "Joe", had convinced me that Mom had eyes behind her head. But one afternoon I decided to run away from home, not knowing that Mom was inside watching my every move. I walked slowly down the road to this place we called the draining place, about a block from the house, and I hung out at the draining place for about one hour. Night was approaching, and I moved slowly back towards the house, until I ended up on the back porch. Mom then came out to let me back in the house. She asked me if I was ready to obey and stop acting like a spoiled brat. The one thing I learned from this ordeal was that Mom did not give in when she was pressured. Some of my friends at school talked about getting what they wanted when they ran away. But that did not work with my Mom. She didn't know I only wanted to spend the weekend with a classmate, not to leave home.

Growing up with a lot of sisters and brothers made life very interesting. I learned a lot of short cuts merely by observing my older siblings grow up. I avoided many bumps in the road and punishments, because I knew not to go their routes or not to make the same old mistakes they made. Growing up my hair was long, it was shoulder length. Totsie always combed and hot pressed my hair. I remember when I was five years old, it was close to Easter Sunday, and Totsie curled my ponytails and cut me some bangs. I felt like a big girl, but Mom did not approve of it. At first she was very upset. Mom did not want her little girl to grow up too fast, and I recall her saying so. But from then on I could manage my own hair, and I began to comb and style it all by myself. My skin was always fair, but very sensitive to insect bites. My legs would break out with all these dark spots. This made me feel embarrassed when I was in public, because I was thinking my legs looked ugly and everyone that saw me thought the same thing. My irritated skin soon affected my personality, and this continued throughout my teenage years. In my early twenties, I started to save my money to seek medical help from a Dermatologist. When I got enough money saved, I made an appointment with a Dermatologist in Little Rock, Arkansas. So the skin treatments begun, and periodically I visited the specialist. No, it did not go well at first, in fact, my legs got worse because I was allergic to an agent in the steroid injections that was administered to me. Yes, I had to deal with the process of stepping down off of the injections and fighting the infection at the same time. This ordeal went on for about three to four months, but finally; my legs were healed. I thank God for giving the doctor wisdom and for His divine intervention. This was by far the hardest battle I had to fight during my teenage years and in my early twenties. Although this was a major struggle in my life, I thank God for salvation at an early age which kept me sound.

In our family we some how bonded together in groups or in pairs. My brother, Frederick, called "Bobby" was next to me and he loved following me around. Not that we had very many places that we could wander off to, but it was the idea that we did it together. This was fun because I learned how to hang tough with the boys. I swung on the monkey vines, rolled down the hill inside barrels, climbed trees, jumped off buildings, waded in the muddy ditches after the rain, and rolled marbles in the dust. You name it and we just about did it. Those were the days when children stayed outside all day and played. Mom didn't worry if we were alright or if we were safe; unless we stayed in the woods too long, then she would call for us to get back in the yard. As we grew older, there were times I thought it was not cool for my little brother to be following me around all. Mom's brother, Uncle Homer, would tease us all the time. When he saw Bobby going somewhere without me, he would say, "Come on Bora", that was my nick name. Yes he was right, immediately when Bobby realized I was not on his heels he would call for me to COME ON! It was like we were joined at the hip or something. Although we were almost twins, because it was only eleven months difference in our ages. Separatism was pretty painful for Bobby, but I started being too girlish for him. Even as young teenagers, we would compete in school work and at home in the kitchen cooking. I remember when Mother agreed for me to bake my first cake. Bobby was watching every step, and from that moment on he wanted to bake the next cake. We only had desserts on weekends, so we sure didn't have any ingredients to waste. He had to really convince Mom that he could do this, and he did. His first cake turned out better than my first one. We both became very good cooks and very good competitors. Bobby and I were both good in Typewriting and in Shorthand. He tried hard to bet me in everything I did. One day Dad bought Bobby a motorcycle. I thought it was a pretty cool ride, so I would ride on the back with him, until one day I talked him into letting me take the driver seat. I did okay for a short time, but later I forgot how to shift down all the gears. I panicked when the bike jumped and I ran right into my sister, Betty's little white car we called "RickaSha". Boy was she upset, and needless to say, that ended my motorcycle driving career.

I guess it paid off in more than one way, my being a little tomboy as a kid. I learned how to stand up to the bullies, and also how to defend myself. My cousins down the road would come out to play with us, and before the games were over the boys would always try to cheat on the girls. Arthur Holt's two daughters, Wilma and Winnie; Cousin Gracie Lamb's daughter, Evelyn; my sister Rose Mary and I; were considered the Girl Team. My brothers, Bobby and Larry, Rosie Lee (Holt) Tolliver's three sons; Sonny, Patrick and Melvin, were considered the Boy Team. We would be having so much fun until Evelyn's big brother, John Jr. popped in. He would always mess up things. Whenever we were playing, he was always stirring up trouble and annoying all of the smaller kids. Jr. was too old to be playing with us, but I guess he felt left out since there were no other boys around his age. Yes, it was me that would always fight him off, that's if I could catch up with him. He could run really fast, but so could I. I would bite him, kick him, and I remember once hitting him with a big brick. I got counseled by Mom for throwing that brick. I learned better from

Mom's first warning. Mom's second warnings were by no means just talking it was action, if you know what I mean. I have never seen so many shoes worn out.

Yap, I was little Miss Independent. But of course, that came with much discipline. God blessed Bobby and me through our closeness we had grown up together. Today you can see several manifestations that came from us being close knit, and from having loving parents that took the time with us. They also understood us as children and disciplined us. Lord knows I needed it.

I was pretty strong in mind and in body as a teenager. I remember one Saturday afternoon when my oldest brother, Joe, was fixing his old car. It was light blue and white, and a terrible thing happened. The car fell down on him crashing his collarbones. He was lying helpless calling for somebody please help him. Mother was in the house getting dress to go to town for groceries. We were calling for her to come, saying, "Joe is hurt". It didn't matter if she got her clothes on or not; she came running outside. I knew this was very bad when Mom starting crying, "Lord Jesus help me…help me now!" I grabbed the back fender of that old car and I lifted it up for a little while. Then someone got the tractor and raised it up until he was pulled out from underneath. Mother threw on some clothes and got Joe to the hospital. Thank God he made it through the operations, and all the procedures it took for his bones to mend. Again, my faith in God was getting stronger and stronger. God gave me strength to lift that heavy car off my big brother. Mother was always praying and instilling the Word of God in us. We learned at an early age that God hears and answers our prayers. Mother would always say, "This is not a laughing matter, when you pray you be sincere". Thank God for his grace and mercy. I accepted him at the age of fourteen. It is so awesome to walk in the path of righteousness.

My spiritual life began to grow, and yes I had many challenges. I was very opinionated, and had to learn early in life that we walked by faith and not by site. My older sisters and my Mom were my mentors. I began to read my Bible, and to fast and pray just like they were doing. The youth revivals were so powerful that I would rather go to church than eat. We were receiving God's spiritual food and my soul was getting fat. I loved to hear my Mom and the older Saints sing songs unto God. They would sing until God's presence filled that little dusty country church, as they shouted and praised God with all their might. My sister, Betty, was used by God so miraculously in leading the youth at our local church and in our church district. Eventually, she was appointed positions in the State Youth Department. We loved it when she took us to the Youth meetings. We participated in all of the activities that were going on in the District, State, and also in the National church. We developed so much faith from watching Mom, and being taught the Word of God correctly. I remember leading a song with our District Choir, in a State Youth Congress in Pine Bluff. I know that was God in me, because normally I am pretty shy about getting in front of a group of people. I guess I experienced Holy Boldness! I was born on the twenty ninth of July and I am bold as a LION not because of a horoscope symbol but because God's word said I could be.

Elder Clarence Guydon was my pastor for many years from the time I was saved until his passing in January 2001. He was also my brother-in-law, and such an incredible man. He loved his family and his church family, as well; he was married to my third oldest sister, Demetrice. He took his time teaching us the Word of God, while making it plain. He would always express how important it was to stay awake and listen to the Word and receive it, because we were going to need it one day. I can remember one night at church I just could not keep my eyes open and he suggested that I stand up, so I could wake up. I was so ashamed. After that, I tried extremely hard not to go to sleep in church ever again. Elder Guydon went off to college to get a better education to get a good job to provide for his family. I moved in with Demetrice and the four children to help out while he was gone through the week, because they only had one car. Their oldest child, Veronica had started school and would ride the school bus in the afternoon to Grandma's house. After work I would pick her up, and we would head home down that dusty road. We had lots of fun. I experienced a lot, living under the same roof with the Guydons. I even got married while

I was living with the Guydons. I had gotten so attached to Veronica, John, Mary, and Charles, until it was very hard leaving them; and going off with this soft spoken man I had fallen in love with, none other but Mr. Paul Edward Brown.

Paul and I were married on May 26, 1979. Elder Guydon performed the Ceremony, blessed our union, and sent us on our way. Paul was such a gentleman. He was very careful not to hurt my feelings. We loved the church and listening to Bible tapes, and listening to the William Brothers' songs. March 29, 1980 we had our first born son, Edward Marcell. His birth did not go as planned. An emergency operation was performed and he was very sick. The medical staff moved very quickly, and my baby was rushed to another hospital from where I was. He was taken to St. Vincent and I was told that it was the best Prenatal Care Facility for critical babies, while I remained at the Doctors Hospital. I did not fear for my baby's life or for my own life, not once. I just rested assured that God was in control and that everything was going to be alright. God totally healed our baby when he was about three months old. Pastor Guydon prayed and asked Paul and me, "If God heals this child, will you remind him when he is of age, what God did?" A big *"YES WE WILL"* came out of our mouths at the same time, and indeed we did. Marcell was very strong as a baby, even at three months old he would raise up on his hands and toes, and let himself down, as though he was doing push-ups. Paul would often tell the family that his baby boy can do push-ups. He would put Marcell on the floor and just say the magic words, "Do your push-ups for daddy" and up he would go to work. I thank God for our families. They were right there by our side the entire time, when those first few months were so difficult. I remember one afternoon Marcell didn't seem to be breathing correctly, I called Lavarange down to the house to check on him and she called the doctor in Little Rock. They told her to bring the baby over to the clinic so they could check him over. Betty went with Lavarange to Little Rock, I was on bed rest and could not take the long ride; but I was pacing the floor until they called me back and said that my baby was fine. He was a little hungry and just wanted more to eat. He downed an entire 6 ounce bottle of baby Gatorade liquid. Marcell had developed a habit during his Pre-natal Care of getting attention very quickly. After all, this was the first week home from the hospital. I was following the doctor's orders which were to elevate him and feed him every two to three hours, not more than two ounces at a time. Just when Paul and I had gotten comfortable with taking good care of Marcell, another surprise was on the way, I was pregnant with our second child. We were a little bit overwhelmed with this news, and quickly prayed for God's protection and divine health of this child. We were strong believers that God would answer our prayers. This pregnancy was much different from the first one and I was not sick the least bit. I worked up to the day the doctor said, "I believe this baby is ready". We had scheduled a date to take the baby, which was April 11, 1981 and on my Moms' birthday. But the doctor was being a little cautious because of my past history he was not going to risk this happening again. I was just there doing a routine office visit on March 17, and that very day my doctor scheduled me to go the hospital the very next day for observation. I tried to convince him to wait until Marcell was at least one year old, that was only eleven more days. All I could think about was Bobby and me, like twins! Upon the next morning, we went to the hospital. I kept thinking, "I'm going to have a baby tomorrow". I just couldn't get over this, no labor pains and I am getting ready for the birth of my second child. We still didn't know if it was a GIRL or BOY. Since we already had a boy, in my head I thought sure this one would be a girl. I was wrong, it was another boy. We named him, Nolan Paul born on March 19, 1981. Naming the boys was somewhat a little struggle with their Dad, **Paul Edward**. He decided that he wanted a Paul Jr. we had already compromised with Marcell, and that is the very reason he has part of his Dad's name. Now with Nolan, he was at it once again… NO…NO…NO…I replied, you just don't name the second boy Jr. (end of sentence). Okay we will use the other part of your name for Nolan and now you have it, you're two little JR's (**Edward Marcell and Nolan Paul**). Nolan was so peaceful and calm when he was born. He was very healthy, weighing in at 8 pounds and 4 ounces. God for sure answered our prayer. Now we have two beautiful babies, and they have parents that love them so much. Paul and I dedicated these boys to the Lord, and asked God to give us the knowledge, wisdom, and understanding, to guide them in the right way. They are definitely a pair, and as ironic as it may sound, they grew up close knitted just like my brother, Bobby and I. They did everything together from sharing toys and books, to playing sports and scouting.

When Marcell turned five years old, he was getting ready to start kindergarten, but little did we know that Nolan was thinking he was going also. We searched around to find a school nursery to put Nolan in, so he was going to school also. Mrs. Starline Johnson had a nursery called, "the Care Bears". This nursery was the perfect one. Nolan loved going to that school. This made him feel just like his big brother, because he was going to school as well. Nolan would like toys that talked, such as Big Bird, Alfa, and Teddy Ruxpin just to name a few. Whenever his brother made him upset, he would get down on the floor with all of his stuffed talking animals, and talk to them about his brother. I think he grew out of that stage, well at least he told me he did.

I remember one winter snowy day I was taking the boys to school, and then I was going to work. A man passed by us speeding and lost control of him vehicle. He made a u-turn and collided head-on with my car. Well, in the ditch we went. The impact caved in my car and broke my ankle. When I saw the steering wheel coming toward my face, all I could do was turn my face to the side. But it still split my jaw. I was also pinned in the car. All I could think about was my boys. I called out to them in the back seat. They were in shock, but alright. I then asked them to get out of the car, but they kept telling me to get out first. I could not move, but I assured them that I would be alright. Finally the ambulance arrived, and so did Paul. After they were able to get me out of the car, I was taken to the hospital. It took a while for my jaw and ankle to heal, but I was blessed. The man driving the other vehicle was not so blessed. My jaw was so swollen and bruised until Nolan would tell me that it looked like I had some of that nasty stuff in my mouth. I thank God for taking care of us.

The boys were both Eagle Scouts. Paul and I were thankful for the survival skills they learned during their camping events. I had never camped out in the woods all night, until I helped with their Troop #260 at Cold Creek in Damascus, Arkansas. I was not good at camping, there were too many bugs, but I made it through it all. Paul and I were very supportive in everything the boys participated in, and we taught them to do their level best in whatever they were involved in. We taught them to always put God first and other things second, and yourself last. Most of the time the boys would say this motto didn't make much sense, but they would try. Paul had an Auto Mechanic Shop next to the house when we lived in Almyra, Arkansas. He was always teaching the boys little things about automobiles. One Saturday afternoon Nolan decided that one the four wheelers was not running right, so he flipped the seat over, took out the engine, worked on it, and put it all back together. Nolan was about six years old at that time. If it had a dial or a knob on it, then his curiosity got the best of him.

God blessed us to buy a piece of commercial land in Stuttgart, in January of 1987. Paul then moved his business to Stuttgart, naming it "Brown's Auto Repair and Service". It is located on Michigan Avenue. Paul has been there for 22 years. He has always enjoyed mechanic work because he knew it like the back of his hand. The boys grew up in and around the shop, and should know how to repair their own vehicles. I have heard shop talk so much, I even know more than most women. I graduated from Philander Smith College in Business, and work as a business analysis for Riceland Foods Incorporation, where I have worked for 37 years. I am the bookkeeper for Mt. Calvary Church, Dew-Baby's Restaurant, and Brown's Auto Repair and Service. I am also on the Board of Trustees for the church, and besides working part time at the restaurant. I think I wear enough hats.

One Sunday evening in May of 1998, Paul and I came home from church and ate dinner. We were relaxing around the house, and waiting on the boys to return from their trip. They spent the week-end with a friend to attend the School Homecoming in Conway, Arkansas. I heard the telephone ringing, but Paul answered the call. The next thing I knew Paul was running through the house rounding up his keys telling me to come on. Then he said the boys were in an accident. I grabbed my keys and followed him, because he was driving the tow truck. We drove about forty miles before reaching the scene and it was a bloody site. There was a crowd of people there. I could hear Mom's voice saying, "Lord Jesus help me now". I sure called on the Lord's help. Both of the boys were in the ambulance, and when I saw them I became weak in my knees. I remembered the Word of God saying, "My seed shall dwell mighty upon the earth", and "When I passed by you and I saw you polluted in your own blood, I say Live." (Ezekiel 16:5) I knew that they were in God's hand. They kept trying to tell me something, and Nolan kept holding my hand. The Chevy blazer SUV had been flipped so many times until it was about flatten. The boys were ejected. One man from the fire department witnessed seeing Marcell flying in the air and into the stop sign, and Nolan being hit by a flying object. They had a friend riding in the back with them, who sustained injuries to his left arm. He was treated at Stuttgart Hospital and released. Marcell and Nolan were taken to Stuttgart Hospital to stabilize them, and then transferred to the trauma center in Little Rock, Arkansas. Nolan only had ½ inch of his eye lid attached. He had six eye surgeries. Marcell had several broken bones; in his head, face, arm, knee, and a broken shaft in his right eye. It is funny how they were laying next to each other in the hospital, but could not see each other. They kept trying, but they couldn't turn that far. This accident happened two weeks before Marcell's graduation. Both of the boys were in the hospital for seven days. Marcell was not able to walk upon discharge, and he was not expected to walk during the time of his graduation. Well, the day of his graduation, he got up and walked. He got a standing ovation as he walked across the stage at his graduation. God took good care of them when the brakes malfunctioned on that Blazer SUV. Mom always said, "God can do anything but fail." The brakes failed, but God did not fail.

After High School, Marcell and Nolan both went off to the same college at University of Arkansas at Little Rock. They lived together in an apartment for a couple of years. Marcell now lives in California, and has done well in his Acting and Modeling career. He is now a top salesperson for Christian Audigier by Ed Hardy, and loving it everyday. Nolan lives in Dallas, Texas, and is presently in management with Chase Mortgage Bank, and is during well with his skills. Nolan has a son, Braxton, who is very much like him. Paul and I spend a lot of time with Braxton, and we love being a Grandma and Papa.

Baby Girl

I am Glenda Hall, born December 19, 1959, at the clinic in Clarendon, Arkansas. I am the last girl in the family, and next to the baby. I was known as the baby until January 27, 1966, when Andre' was born. I remember Momma bringing Andre' home and I was insisting that she take him back. I grieved over losing this position, and was mean to Andre'. I did have an outlet, because Larry and I were inseparable. He always looked out for me, and continued to treat me like the baby. I remember an episode that really caused me to trust God. I was home with Daddy one Saturday, and my brother, Bobby brought Larry home and said that he was not feeling well. Bobby stated that he believed that someone poisoned Larry's drink at the bar. I clearly remember Larry walking toward the refrigerator and falling down as he passed out right before my eyes. Momma was gone, so I couldn't call for her. Momma always said, "Take the Lord along with you everywhere you go because you're going to need Him". Then she said, "You're going to need Him in you home". I rushed over and kneeled down over him, and he was not breathing. I did not know how to perform CPR, so I started praying very fervently for my brother, and calling his life back into his body. It didn't take very long, before Larry started breathing again. This was when I first recall experiencing the miracle working power of God. Our family was strongly affiliated with church, and I had always heard

Momma and others testifying about the power of God; but from that day I knew for myself that God should raise one from the dead. Later on Larry testified that he was dying, and knew that he was not saved at the time. He said that he saw his casket, his spirit had left his body, and he knew this was not good; but he heard me praying and calling him back, and God gave his life back.

I started early going to the cotton fields, but I didn't have to work. My day in the fields consist of playing around and riding on the cotton sacks. Lavern would pull me on her sack a lot, so it was fun for me. Although I was a Daddy's baby, I was a bit spoiled by everybody. I knew my parents and siblings would protect me. One day I was going outside and the rooster attacked me, and I was crying. Momma got that rooster by the neck and twisted it off. I was glad that I did not have to be afraid of going outside anymore.

Momma always would drive fast, and one day I was riding with her down the gravel road, and she was going so fast that she lost control, and off the road we went, and into a deep ditch. Momma was hurt and broke two of her ribs; I was okay physically, but not emotionally. I refused to get in a car for over a month with anyone, and with Momma even longer.

I do not recall getting many spankings, but I do remember Larry getting them a lot. He was always getting into things. However, there was this one isolated incident when Daddy told me to get his bath water ready, but I chose to go next door to play with Cousin Sue. When Daddy figured out that I was defiant, he came over with his belt, and I knew I was in trouble so I ran. I got one lick and that's all I ever needed.

Momma on the other hand, was gone often taking care of business. Momma would forget my birthday, because it is so close to Christmas, and she would start early preparing for Christmas. At that time momma's brethren, Uncle Homer, lived with us. He taught me how to cut up and fry a whole chicken. By the time Momma got home, the chicken was ready to be served. I was very proud of my accomplishment, because I was only 13 years old. I also took advantage of these times, and convinced Larry to teach me how to drive; without Momma knowing of course. Larry was a good teacher, and by the time I was 14 years old; I was a pretty good little driver. Being the baby girl, I didn't have to work as hard as my older sisters; so I took advantage of my position. Arthur's daughter, Jackie, and I were good friend. Until I was eight years old, we would walk down the road, because we lived close to each other. We moved about four miles away when I was eight years old, after our house burned down. We still saw each other at church.

I did alright in school, but I wasn't completely focused. I was on the track team in Junior High School and in High School. I won 1st place in the High School competition against other schools. My picture was in the local Newspaper, and it caught me in action; I was running full speed with my face slightly turned, my mouth slightly opened, and my feet and hands in motion. There was no doubt that I was going for the prize. I later joined the CEO Program at school, landing me a job at Sears in my senior year. I was glad to have my own money, and to buy the things I wanted. I graduated from Stuttgart High School with the class of 1978. I continued working after my graduation.

A year after graduation, I married LeRoy Vincent. He later became a minister, and things were going pretty good. We both were in church, and God was blessing us. We brought a house, and had a nice car. I did not work outside the home. We had our first child February 23, 1981, Tenike, and we continued to be faithful to God and attending church. On December 2, 1983, we had our second child, Brittany. At that point my duties really increased around the house; combing their hair, getting them ready for church, getting LeRoy' things ready, cooking dinner, cleaning up after everyone, and getting myself ready. I think I did a good job. We notice Brittany squinted her eyes whenever she was in the sun light. At five years old, she had to have surgery to remove cataracts, causing her legal blindness in that eye. But thank God, she has no problem seeing out of the other eye. Later on LeRoy and I started having trouble in our marriage. My oldest daughter started complaining of headaches. I was raised up in the church, and was taught that marriages are suppose to last for a lifetime; but it did not work out that way. We ended the marriage in divorce. This did affect the girls, I think it is hard for children to sort out things when divorce is involved; feeling that they have to choose between the two parents. Momma was there for me and kept the children a lot, but this was during the time her memory was deteriorating. This was not an easy road. Tenike developed an addiction, which caused her to be in and out of rehabilitation centers. This was very difficult knowing that I was pleading for help for her long before it got to that point, and it seemed that there was no where to go. Every place that promised, did not deliver. She is out now and progressing; and she looks well. Tenika has two children, Javias McCollough born December 20, 2002, and Skyy Fitzpatrick born February 9, 2006. Brittany has one child Jashua Lowery born August 29, 2003. They are carrying on my nickname daddy gave me, "Boo". So, I am now known as "Grandma Boo Boo". I also went through a period of looking for love in all of the wrong places, because everyone who was in our church is related to me. So I ended up getting married again, but to someone not in the church. I found myself in an abusive marriage that eventually ended up in divorce. This was very hard, coming from a loving and caring home, and experiencing a totally different lifestyle. But considering the fact that we were not brought up to just give up on what we want. I went through a period of sadness and reevaluating my life. Then I simply dusted my self off and tried again. I am back in church, and I am happily married to a former Arkansas Razorback, "Reggie Hall". He is very thoughtful, hard working, and loving. We recently bought a house, and he is always surprising me with things I like as a touch of elegance. We share the same values. We both attend my home church. We pay tithes, and God is blessing us. I give thanks to my God for His mercy. I have been an employee of Lennox for 15 years and counting. I am also part owner and worker of Dew-Baby's Restaurant, named after Momma.

Although we came from a large family, our parents still managed to instill some very important key factors to success. They taught us the true meaning of love, togetherness, and survival. They were truly a God sent gift.

The most recent incident happened a few weeks ago with my brother, Larry. I was called to Stuttgart hospital, because Larry had a blood vessel to burst in his head. When I arrived, they where waiting on a return call from Little Rock. Time went on, and on; until I could not take it any more. I went and ask the doctor if he would please just transport my brother to Little Rock as soon as possible. I told him I was not trying to tell him how to run his business, or tell him what to do; but that was my brother out there, and he just didn't understand. I knew time was of the essence, and Larry was losing consciousness. The doctor then called for the ambulance to transport Larry to Little Rock. Then I went back to Larry, and asked him to squeeze my hand if he understood, and he did. I told him that he would not die, but live, and declare the works of the Lord. I told him to remember that we had been through this before, and God brought him out, and He was going to do the same thing again. Shortly after that, Larry lost consciousness, the ambulance arrived, and transported him to University of Arkansas Medical Center. About 30 hours later, Larry regained consciousness, and later asked, "Where is baby Boo". I give thanks to our great God.

Girstine Jeffery "DewBaby"
April 11, 1920 – May 3, 2007

The Jeffery Family

Front left: Larry Jeffery
First row left: Rose Stovall, George Jeffery, Girstine Jeffery, Andre'
Jeffery, and George Jeffery, Jr.
Middle:Deborah Brown, Glenda Hall, Lavarange Davis, Mary
Ann Wofford, Betty Watkins, Lillie Jeffery
Back left: Juanita Owens, Demetrice Guydon, Fredick Jeffery,
Jewell Wofford, and Pearl St. Clair

Mother Girstine Jeffery at the old home church

LaVergne, TN USA
13 October 2009
160647LV00002B/3/P